HAPPY TIMES IN *Norway*

TRANSLATED FROM THE NORWEGIAN BY

JORAN BIRKELAND

SIGRID UNDSET

HAPPY TIMES

IN

NORWAY

GREENWOOD PRESS, PUBLISHERS
WESTPORT, CONNECTICUT

Library of Congress Cataloging in Publication Data

Undset, Sigrid, 1882-1949.
  Happy times in Norway.

  Translation of Lykkelige dager.
  Reprint of the ed. published by Knopf, New
York.
  I. Title.
PT8950.U5L8413   1979   839.8'2'87203   [B]
ISBN 0-313-21267-8   79-9997

First published October 5, 1942 by Alfred A. Knopf, Inc.,
New York

Reprinted with the permission of Alfred A. Knopf, Inc.

Reprinted in 1979 by Greenwood Press, Inc.
51 Riverside Avenue, Westport, CT 06880

Printed in the United States of America

10 9 8 7 6 5 4 3 2 1

WHEN the Germans invaded Norway on April 9, 1940, the Happy Times in our country came to an end.

The two boys, of whose childhood joys and adversities I have told in this book, were young men by that time. Tulla had died a year before. And, since nobody could have explained to her why all the good things and pleasures she was used to had come to an end—why her dear flag could not fly over her home any more, why there were to be no procession and music on the Seventeenth of May, and no sheaves of grain for the birds outside her window at Christmas, no rides to the mountains in the summer, no sledges with bells in the winter—it was a good thing that she was dead. She was spared the sufferings inflicted upon her people by a nation who has deemed children like her—not able to achieve anything in this world except teaching us love and tenderness, and giving love and tenderness in return—unfit to live.

On that black ninth of April Anders and Hans escaped from occupied Oslo. Next morning they both joined the Norwegian army near Lillehammer. Three weeks later Anders was killed in action, up in his home valley. Hans finally joined his mother in Sweden, went with her all the way through Russia, Siberia, Japan, to America. But when the Norwegian army was being re-formed somewhere in Great Britain, he returned to the colors. By the time this book has been printed he may have had the opportunity he wished for, to fight again for his king and native land. When he said good-bye to Mother in the Grand Central Terminal, to travel to the secret port where his ship waited, he told her: "You know, Mother, if we get our country back again from the Germans, nothing matters. And if not, and if you and I should have to live nevertheless, we must acknowledge that Anders was the only lucky one in our family."

But we Norwegians know for certain that we shall have our country back again, free and swept clean of the forces of evil. What if the fine old farms up along the river in our valley of Gudbrandsdal, and all our other valleys, are burnt down; what if ever so many of our men are dead on battlefields and in prisons; what if the courteous and happy hard-working peasantry of Norway have been impoverished—deprived of their horses and cows that were as dear to the owners as if they were members of the family; what if the Germans have destroyed the fruits of centuries of labor and millenniums of cultural development—we still have our land. We are still the same people who built it up, to be a place where human dignity and integrity were cherished, where friendliness, happiness and charity were considered the best things in life.

Some day—maybe soon—we will be able to unfurl our flag over every home in Norway—or over the ruins of homes to be rebuilt. Some day, little children and gawky youngsters in high school will march in procession, with flags flying and music playing our national hymns, on the Seventeenth of May. And some time—maybe sooner, maybe later than we expect—we will be able again to offer up to the wild birds of our woods and mountains the sheaf of grain at Christmas in front of our windows—the sacred gift of some thousands of years of Norwegian history to the powers of life and fertility, whatever name our ancestors gave to the Good Spiritual Forces watching over our home. And on that day, when we can again hoist the Christmas sheaves of grain at our front doors, we will finally know that Happy Times in Norway have returned to the land of our forefathers and our children.

Sigrid Undset.

Brooklyn, May 17, 1942.

CONTENTS

PART I

MERRY CHRISTMAS

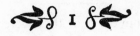

"POTATO-DIGGING VACATION" BEGAN WITH RAIN AND ended with rain, and the boys were bored and cross. They could not find anything to do themselves, and nothing that Mother and Thea suggested was any fun.

"You ought to be ashamed of yourselves," Thea said. "In the country the children have to go out and dig potatoes rain or shine. You don't even do so much as help straighten up the garden for your mother."

What she said was so true. At all the farms around the little town, grownups and children alike were out in the muddy potato fields, bent over the long rows of potato vines, with gunny sacks over their heads to ward off the pouring rain.

But Anders and Hans were unimpressed. It had always been impossible to interest either of them in gardening, though Thea kept telling them early and late how children in the country had to make themselves useful from the time they were only knee high to a grasshopper. *She* had had to, when she was little. The boys knew that what she said was true, for many of their schoolmates lived on farms.

But between potato-digging and Christmas, there was not one single holiday—except Sundays, of course. And Anders claimed he could remember one year when it had snowed so early they could go skiing at potato-digging time.

"Don't you remember, Mother? It was that time I was supposed to be in the school ski contest, and when I came to say good-by to you, you pulled down that scarf I had over my face and saw the measles I had got during the night."

Mother said he must be mistaken. There had never been snow on the ground here as early as potato-digging, and besides, the school ski contest was always in January, so that act he was so proud of—trying to sneak off skiing when he had measles—certainly must have taken place at some other time of the year. At potato-digging time it *always* rained—practically.

And it continued to rain and rain. The boys came home from school looking like two bedraggled crows.

"Go up and change," Mother said. "Socks too."

"And underwear," added Thea. "Here, let me see—"

She pulled down Hans's breeches to confirm the fact that yes, indeed, his underwear was wet from top to bottom. Anders was so big now she could not very well investigate him that way but, judging from his brother's state . . .

"Will Madam tell Anders that he also must change his underwear?"

And then Thea would be cross with them for throwing their wet clothes all over their room and leaving pools and puddles everywhere—on the floor, on the chairs, on the beds, and even on their school books on the table, so that they got spotted and spoiled. As if the boys' books were not spotted enough already! And then to have to try to dry out all those things in front of stoves and to have their heavy boots hanging over the kitchen range. . . . "Oh," Thea sighed, "what a mess!" . . . And every morning when the boys started to school Thea had to run and catch them at the door, for they always forgot their oilskin slickers. Then she would discover that the slickers were covered with mud, and she would have to get a damp cloth and wipe them off before she could let the boys go. So they were late for school, because of *that*, though on other days they were usually late for some other reason.

The drone of the waterfalls in the forest became

louder day by day. From the bedrooms upstairs the river's plunging, fall after fall, down over the wooded ridge east of town could nearly always be heard. Only in midsummer was its voice hushed, and even then it could be heard drumming after a rain if there were a southerly breeze.

One morning white mist-smoke rose over the fir and spruce tops over Hellgate. The next day a broad band lay from the ridge top clear down to the bridge in Main Street. On Sunday it lifted a little, and Mother suggested that they take a walk to the river to see how high it was. Anders, who in sheer desperation had hauled out all his mathematics books, was studying for his entrance examination at Christmas. Mathematics was the only subject he found any fun. But Hans was not one to seek comfort in schoolbooks and he was ready at once to go with Mother.

They clambered over the fence at the garden's farthest end and took the path across the fields. The path was underwater and they had to hop and leap from one mound to another, and every time Hans slid and splashed into the path he howled with delight. Occasionally Mother would plump into it too, and then he would howl even more ecstatically.

"Now *you* got wet, Mother! What do you think Thea will say now?"

For an instant the sun peeped from behind a cloud bank, shining goldenly into the little puddles and making the naked birch and the newly washed dark-green fir boughs glisten. Yes, it was beautiful, but . . .

"Just think, Hans! Only one month today until Christmas Eve."

"You will have to begin reading to me soon, mother. About Jesus being born. . . ."

Mother always read the Christmas story to her younger son just before Christmas.

"Say, mother, you probably know it by heart, don't you? You could *tell* it to me now. Then you wouldn't have to read it to me tonight after I have gone to bed, and you could read me an adventure story instead."

Of course it was only admirable that Hans was both pious and practical.

Mother began telling the story. Hans thrust his little fist into her hand, for now they had reached the road, and the walking was easier than it had been along the footpath in the field.

". . . and there were some shepherds, you see, watching over their flocks . . ."

"And they were drunk," Hans interjected, tense and enraptured.

"Are you crazy, child!" Mother exclaimed, horrified. "Of course they were not drunk. How can you say

7

such a thing? They were unusually good and pious men."

"Yes, Mother. But men who stay out in the fields all night are always drunk."

There was Prohibition in Norway in those years, after the First World War. And to everyone, down to the tiniest urchin, violators of the alcoholic liquor law were enormously exciting topics of conversation. Before Mother could pick up where she had left off, and continue the Bible story, Hans remarked thoughtfully:

"The prodigal son you read about one time, mother, he was out at night too because he had got so bad, drinking and carousing. Don't you remember? Where do you think he got the stuff, by the way? From the Pharisees?"

"No, no. The Pharisees were just the opposite. The trouble with them was that they were altogether too particular about obeying all the laws, and so on."

"Phewy! I'll bet they were just putting on, mother. It was probably just because they were always carrying on themselves that they were always fighting with the Customs."

That the stories he heard during Religious Instruction had taken place in gray antiquity was not clear to Hans. Father Sund had been considerably astonished that day when he was telling the children about Adam and Eve being expelled from Paradise.

"Now they've opened a beauty parlor in Main Street," Hans had announced. "Poor Eva. Well, she probably had to do whatever she could to make her living."

A new beauty parlor had just opened in town and it was called "Eve."

They were almost there. Mist from the falls came driving toward them, wetting them through and through, and over the spruce tops rose and fell the mighty, pale-gold column of water where the flooded river charged against the cliff wall in Hellgate. It was impossible to talk any more; one could not hear one's own voice for the roar of the falls. But Hans shrieked to heaven in glee. The little bathing house at the dam below the falls lay swirling round and round in the streaming dark-yellow water. Slowly, slowly, it was drifting toward the brink. It tottered—tipped, and then disappeared in the boiling white foam—to bob up in splinters an instant later farther down the stream. Hans, wild with excitement at seeing something destroyed, ran down alongside.

Beneath the wet, dripping branches, white and grayish-white mushrooms were growing—whole little forests of them, with pine needles and bits of litter clinging to their slippery, wet caps. But they were good and fresh, and Mother and Hans picked so many they had to use Mother's windbreaker as a kind of basket in which to carry them. That deliciously fragrant odor of woods and moss and fresh mushrooms!

"I'll bet Mother's feet are wet now. She's much wetter than I," Hans shouted in jubilation as Thea came and unlatched the gate for them.

"Shouldn't Madam go up and change, *at once?*" Thea said in a highly suggestive tone. "Madam should not forget to change her stockings as well," she called after them.

For their supper the boys had what they liked best in all the world—crisp bacon curls and mushrooms sautéed in bacon fat.

Anders took the dogs out, and when he came in, he reported that the stars were out—well, at least there were openings in the clouds where he could see *some* stars. Perhaps there would be frost tonight.

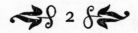

THE NEXT MORNING THE WEATHER WAS THE SAME, EX-
cept that the rain had thickened into sleet, but now and
then a few wet, gray snow splotches fell to earth. It was,
at least, *snow*. Later in the day, large soft flakes appeared, the garden turned white, and the tree branches
began to bow under a burden of heavy, wet snow.

The boys leaped to life. They got their skis down
from the storehouse attic and began overhauling them,
and soon the whole house smelled of turpentine and
tar from various mixtures of ski grease Anders had
warming—and boiling over—in tin cups on the kitchen
stove.

The next morning the fog was so thick one could not
see farther than the nearest birches. Of the snow nothing remained but a few strips of slush along the garden's edge!

Now Mother and Thea became infinitely weary of

this endless rainy weather. For it was time to begin the Christmas preparations in earnest. In Norway Christmas is celebrated for thirteen days, and in order that wives and mothers and maids shall not have too much to do during the holiday season, it is the custom to cook and store many different kinds of food and bake heaps of cookies in advance. That way there is always something on hand when guests drop in who must be asked to stay for dinner or for the evening meal. This year Mother had ordered a whole pig, a sheep, and half a reindeer, for she expected a houseful of guests at Christmastime. If the weather is very cold, one needs only to pack down in tubs of snow the meat that is to be eaten fresh. But if the weather is mild—ah, then what a job! Some of the roasts must be partly pre-cooked, other cuts peppered and salted down, pork sausages and blood puddings fried and baked and laid down in crocks that are then sealed over with fat. Besides this, all the other work must be done before Christmas—the pork hams laid in the salt tubs, the mutton hams sugar-cured, and headcheese made from the head and feet. Then the cookies must be baked. And besides all this there is a big washing to be done, and the Christmas house cleaning everywhere.

Thea began with the kitchen. Mari Moen came to do the washing. Mari was from up the valley—a tall, straight-backed old woman with handsome features and dark hair streaked with gray. She had the quietly distinguished air that Norwegian peasant women usually have, and everyone in the house was glad when she came. Thea saw to it that each day one of Mari's favorite dishes appeared for dinner and when Mari was doing a big wash, Anders remembered, for a change, that as a Boy Scout he was duty-bound to help with the work at home. He carried the heavy baskets of wet clothes up from the basement for her and hung them out to dry in the back yard. As far as the other women in the household were concerned, Anders confined himself to saying he would prepare dinner someday, so they could see for themselves he had learned how to broil steak at the Boy Scout camp. Neither Mother nor Thea was eager to have him carry out his promise.

It was well enough to hang out the wash, but how was it to dry before Christmas? Anders and Mari finally had to carry it to the attic and hang it up there.

Suddenly one morning the fog split open. White swirls of mist began to wheel past a pale, glimmering sun that made the millions of waterdrops on the birches around the house glisten and gleam. For the first time in weeks, one could see the dark forested ridges around the town and get a glimpse of the pale sea at the base of the hills. Beyond the garden hedge, in Lysgaard field, the horses were munching at the dead grass. Thea came up from the kitchen garden with a small bowl of freshly grown lettuce, and in the rock garden Hans found three full-blown pansies and some white *Arabis*. It was rather amusing in a way, but not as it should be at Christmastime in Norway.

And Tulla was so cross and restless. The phonograph was kept going all day, playing Christmas carols and marches for her, but neither Mother nor Thea had time to take her walking, or driving in the car, so she was peevish and restless.

Poor little Tulla. She had been ill ever since she was a year old and no doctor had been able to say for certain what ailed her. Now she was ten—three years younger than Anders and three years older than Hans. She could say only a few words and she could not help herself at all. There had to be someone with her constantly to care for her. That was why she was the pet of the entire household. When Mother came up from her workroom to rest, she would always take Tulla on her lap and sing to her. Thea cared for her as if she were a little princess, and the boys built houses of blocks just to give her the pleasure of tearing them down. For Tulla liked everything that tumbled and clattered.

It looked as if the cats too loved Tulla, for the moment they came into the living room they jumped into her lap as she sat in her armchair. Sissi usually paid only a short visit, but Sissi was a pampered darling, with her long, silky, black, white, and chestnut hair. She was one who always knew what she wanted. The dogs, Njord and Neri, were scared to death of her and she could put strange dogs and cats out of her garden in a jiffy. Her own son, Sissyfos, did not dare to come into the kitchen when his mother was there, for she could not bear to have him even look in the direction of the cat dish. The warmest spot under the stove and the softest sofa pillow were Sissi's prerogatives and her private possessions. And when Tulla pulled her fur, or burrowed her fingers into Sissi's ears—Tulla did not realize she hurt the animals when she did things like that—Sissi drew slowly away, wholly in an attitude of self-defense, jumped down and crawled under the stove. She never scratched Tulla, though she took little from anyone else without showing her claws.

But when Tulla took Sissyfos and lifted him up by the tail, he merely closed his eyes and laid back his ears. When she let him go, he hopped right back into her lap again, cuddled up and began to purr. It almost seemed as though he liked to have Tulla handle him so cruelly. True, Sissyfos was the laziest tomcat on earth, Thea said. She claimed she had seen a mouse run right across his nose without bringing even a flick of his whiskers. But the boys thought it was because he was so dreadfully fond of Tulla that he let her do as she liked with him.

Sissi belonged to Hans. He got her when she was a tiny kitten and he was very proud of her, for everyone wanted Sissi's kittens; they were always spoken for far in advance. Sissyfos had been promised to someone, but, as it turned out, the people who were to have him could not take him. Meanwhile he had grown so big that Mother did not have the heart to let him be killed. Besides, he was a very pretty cat—his body chestnut, his chest and boots white. But since he belonged to no one specifically and because it was more or less of an accident that he had stayed on, he was somehow less distinguished than his mother.

The dogs were Mother's, of course. They were of that pedigree known as Norwegian collie, resembling an elkhound, and no dogs were ever more faithful. But they were rather snappish toward strangers, and it was useless for anyone to try to teach them dog tricks. And they were obstinate creatures with their own opinions as to what constituted a dog's function. Njord was four years old, lively and spunky, and everyone said that if Mother would exhibit him at the spring show he would certainly take first prize. Neri was still only a pup, and he did not show off well. Even though he did have such a magnificent pedigree, he did not look exactly as a collie should. His legs were too long and his hair too thin. Nor did his tail have quite the proper arch. But Anders had lost his heart to Neri when he first arrived, a tiny puppy, from the farm up the valley where he was born. He was so young that he lay in his basket and whimpered all night. Poor thing, he was used to lying snug and warm beside all his sisters and brothers close under his mother's body. Anders thought the little puppy was freezing, and lifted him up into bed with him. There Neri found a nice, soft place to sleep, sucking Anders's finger every night until he had become used to his new family. And now Neri himself probably believed he was Anders's dog, for it was at Anders's heels he followed when the boys were home; and when Neri made an ass of himself and tried to play with Sissi's tail, and got spat upon and had a swipe taken at his nose, it was to Anders that he fled, whimpering and complaining that Sissi had been mean to him.

No one can understand how Tulla knows. Days and months do not exist in her little world—but nevertheless, she *always* knows when it is getting along toward a red-letter day in her life—her birthday, Christmas, and the Seventeenth of May. Now she knew Christmas was coming and every year before Christmas Mother had always taken her for a sleigh ride through town to see Main Street decorated with arches of fir and spruce boughs and with colored lights strung from one end to the other, the shops all aglitter with Christmas displays. But this year Tulla *could not* have her sleigh ride—and an automobile ride was not the same. Auto rides were for every day. And there was no use pointing out to Tulla that when there was no *snow* . . .

Tulla was angry, and all in vain was every effort of Mother and Thea and the boys to get her in good humor.

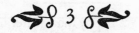

THE NIGHT BEFORE LITTLE CHRISTMAS EVE, THEA AND
Mother worked in the kitchen until long after midnight. The headcheeses and the pigs' feet had been
stowed in the brine, the last cooky boxes were closed
and carried up to the little storage closet, and Thea had
set the sponge for bread and coffeecake. Now she had
thrown open the window to rid the kitchen of its cooking smells.

"Does Madam see? I really think it is beginning to
freeze."

They went out on the stoop. The sky was black and
filled with sparkling stars. They stepped down into the
garden to feel the soil—yes, it was beginning to set.
There was a crackling under their feet as they walked
and Njord, who had slipped out with them, raced as if
shot from a cannon, clear to the foot of the garden, to
bark wildly at absolutely nothing out on the road, only

to show that he was happy that winter had really come.

The hillside was white with frost next morning. Mother was going downtown to the market place, and Hans and Tulla were allowed to go along in the car. The market place was crowded with farmers selling wood, Christmas trees, and sheaves of grain. Hans was allowed to help Mother choose a Christmas tree and to pick out the handsomest sheaves of yellow, heavy-headed grain.

It is the custom in Norway to put a sheaf of grain outside the windows at Christmastime. Thousands of years ago the Stone Age people in Norway, when they had learned to grow grain, believed that the spirit that lived in the earth, and made things grow, fled when the grain was cut. It hid, they thought, in the last remaining stalks, and when these had been cut down, this spirit of growth was thought to be imprisoned in them. That was why the peasants laid aside the last sheaf and kept it. In midwinter, when the earth was frozen hard and covered with snow, and there was a frightening drumming at night from the ice on the sea, and trees cracked in the cold, and it was dark nearly all day—and daylight lasted only that short while from the time the sun, looking ill and feverishly red, crept up over the edge of the forest to hang low over the earth a short while, before dropping down to hide itself again

—then the Stone Age people fetched this last sheaf of grain and hung it near the place they lived. The spirit in it helped the sun become strong again, and once more warm and light the earth to triumph over evil winter. Then the spirit returned to the thawing fields to bring the people a new harvest of blessed grain. . . .

From Asia came stories about powerful gods that ruled life on earth and the fate of men. The one who ruled over the heavens they called Ty, or Ull the Magnificent. One they spoke of only as the Lord— Fröy or Baldr—who ruled over the fertility of the earth and saw to it that animals and mankind had offspring. Sometimes he showed himself to people in the form of a boar with golden tusks and golden bristles. That was why swine came to be sacred and why people sacrificed swine to the god of fertility when at midwinter they tried to influence the powers that would bring back spring. Ever since it has been the custom in Norway to slaughter a pig for Christmas—and thus they do to this day.

But the best god of all was Thor. With that heavy hammer of his he slew trolls and evil things that wanted to wreck the settled countryside. Thor always heard the promises brides and bridegrooms gave each other, and all the bargains and agreements men made. Traitors, liars, and faithless ones could be sure that someday Thor's revenge would smite them. His wife was Sif, with the golden hair that one sometimes saw flashing on the horizon just before Thor came driving in his chariot across the vaulted sky, as thunder boomed and the rain streamed. . . .

Thus, as though Norwegians still believed in gods and goddesses, they kept up the custom of hanging out the sheaf of grain for the midwinter feast. It could mean a sacrifice to the golden-haired Sif, and, besides, the old people had always done it and it had always helped to bring a good year.

There came a time when Norwegians sailed out in their ships along all the European coasts, plundering and burning and murdering wherever they went. But it happened—in England, in Ireland, and in France— that great kings rose up and succeeded in defending their countries from the pirates of the North. Many of the Vikings fell and Norwegians worried about the souls of those men who died in foreign lands and could not be buried in the mounds where their ancestors lay, on the old farms in Norway. Nor did they get the sacrifices and gifts that were supposed to assure them peace after death. The Saxons in Germany believed in a demon, Wotan the Terrible, who, when the storms howled at night and the clouds rolled across the sky, rode at the head of the train of these unhappy and homeless dead. The Vikings chose him to be their god and called him Odin, but only the warriors and chieftains worshiped him. The people at home, who struggled to win for themselves food from the earth and out of the sea, clung to Thor, the peasants' god and protector.

Many young Norwegian princes set out as Vikings and came home Christians, eager to convert all the people to faith in the White Christ. The last of them, Olav Haraldson, succeeded. When he fell at Stiklestad in 1030, he had made Norway a Christian land, and he came to be remembered as Saint Olav.

But the Christian Norwegians kept up the custom of hanging out the Christmas sheaf. Only now they offered it as a gift to the little birds that ventured up to the houses when the snow was so deep in the mountains and in the forests that they could no longer find anything to eat. For Norwegian peasants, or farmers have always loved all living creatures. Christmas night they used to go out to the stable and give the horse and cows and goats and sheep an extra feeding: "Eat and drink, my good cow. Our Lord is born tonight."

So from the earliest times we know anything about our country, even until the Germans came, overrunning and plundering it, a sheaf of grain has been set out for the little birds at every home at Christmas.

Mother always bought so many sheaves that one was set up in front of every window in the house. And when Tulla had got her sheaf set up, she forgot to be cross about the sleigh ride she did not get. She thought it great fun to sit and look at the birds come flying—the nimble yellowhammer, the fat and gluttonous greenfinch people had nicknamed "The Swede," and the bullfinch with its black eyes and its breast as red as a rose in the snow.

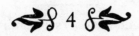

IN NORWAY IT IS CHRISTMAS EVE THAT IS THE GREAT
est and the most sacred time in all the year. To Anders
and Hans, Christmas Eve started in the morning, when
the tree was carried into the large parlor where the fireplace was and Thea brought all the boxes of Christmas
tree trimmings down from the attic. The boys became
very busy wrapping up their presents and writing the
names on the outside—getting their fingers and their
jerseys inky—while Mother was downstairs trimming
the tree. Every once in a while the boys found an ex-
cuse to slip down.

"Mother, how does Charlotte spell her name?"

Actually, what they wanted was to peep at the tree
and see all the old things once more. The little porce-
lain angel, on the tip of the tree, which Grandfather
and Grandmother had got from Grandfather's parents
in Trondheim when Mother was having her first

Christmas tree and was only six months old. Every year some of the Christmas tree decorations broke and Mother added new ones—and Anders could remember which were the old, the older, and the oldest.

The last thing Thea baked was the special Christmas cookies. When they had come out of the oven and lay on the table in rows, big and round and brown, dotted with raisins and candied lemon peel, coffee was served in the living room to the entire household, for on Christmas Eve dinner is always late. But Mother and Thea had to keep leaving the coffee table, for every once in a while someone came—the grocery boy with the latest purchases from the market, or boys from the greenhouses. For at Christmas friends and acquaintances all send flowers to one another, and soon so many bouquets and flowerpots—each containing several kinds of flowering plants—had come that it was hard to find room for them all. And each delivery boy had to have a gift. Anders had volunteered to keep an eye on the mailbox down the road and give the postman, when he turned up, the envelope with his Christmas gift in it.

"It's much colder now," Anders reported as he came in. "The air smells of snow."

Christmas Eve dinner is at six o'clock and it is always rice porridge, boiled codfish, and red wine. At heart,

the boys are not terrifically fond of either the rice porridge or that sour red wine. But that was what *they* had
for Christmas Eve dinner in their home, because
Mother's father had always had porridge and boiled
codfish in *his* home. In many places in Norway people
have clung to the customs of Catholic times and fasted
thus on Christmas Eve, even though it was four hundred years since the country became Protestant. But
Christmas Eve is always festive, for everyone dresses
for dinner or comes to the table dressed in his very best,
and the electric lights are turned off everywhere in the
house, for this night there must be only the living light
of candles, and there must be a candle in every nook
and cranny.

The table was decorated with flowers and candles
stood in the old English-plate candlesticks, and on the
table around these Thea had laid a garland of spruce
fir sprigs and heads of grain. And with a lot of sugar
and cinnamon on it, and a lump of butter in the middle,
the rice porridge did not taste so bad after all. Besides,
there was always one almond in it, and the one who
found the almond in his porridge would have luck all
year. Originally it was probably the custom that the one
who found the almond in his porridge got an extra
Christmas gift. But Grandfather had the idea that his
children should be reared to feel greater joy in giving

than in receiving, so he decided that whichever one of his little girls found the almond should be allowed to be the first to pass out her gifts. Mother said she could not remember that Grandfather's beautiful thought was any too well received by herself and her sisters, so she decided that the almond should simply mean good luck in the new year.

And Tulla sat and was so happy that she laughed loudly all the time, and then everyone felt happy "for her little sake," as Hans put it. Tulla liked rice porridge and even more she liked to watch the candle's flames blaze and flutter when she blew on them. And it was Tulla who raised her head to listen, and said "ding-dong, ding-dong." . . . Tulla was the first to hear the bells ringing Christmas in.

And now everyone took his glass of red wine and went out on the steps.

It was the church bells that were ringing and, as there was a light breeze, they could clearly hear the little bell in Vingrum chapel on the other side of the lake. The night was bright with stars and lights shone from all the windows in the neighborhood. All over the forested ridges, there were pinpoints of light where a farm lay. They stood awhile looking and listening— and then they all raised their glasses and wished one another "Merry Christmas." Hans took his drop of red wine in one gulp, as if it were medicine, for it tasted sour to him, although he would not admit he did not like wine.

And now it was time for Mother to go down to the large parlor and light the Christmas tree. Then it was *really* Christmas. Astonishing, how it could seem just as solemnly wonderful year after year, Mother thought. In the big fireplace a large blaze of resinous pine knots cast a flickering red light across the pine-paneled walls that were smooth as silk to the touch and mellow with age, and brightened the gilded picture frames and the old brown bookbindings with the faded gold printing. The candles on the Christmas tree and the candles in the two old chandeliers that had once hung in a church were mirrored in the windows, where the night pressed blackly against the panes. There was the good odor of fir boughs and melted wax, of lily of the valley, and of hyacinth. Mother moved her chair close to Tulla's, and Anders read the Christmas story for them. In the very middle he was interrupted by Neri, who began to whimper and whine to be taken on his lap. The pup was frightened by all these strange goings on. . . . Household pets dislike anything that upsets their routine. Both cats had left the house early in the afternoon; they did not like the look of things indoors. . . And Neri continued to be restless. Only Njord sat quiet beside the basket of gifts, sniffing longingly at it. He remembered from previous Christmases that there was a package in it for him—a big sausage—and his nose told him it was there again this year.

There were not so many gifts in the Christmas basket this year. Those members of the family who were in Oslo and Stockholm wished to bring their gifts with them when they came up day after next, or Second Christmas Day. And Anders had got his new skis early, so that he could have them in readiness the moment there was some snow. Tulla's fur coat and Swedish sleigh were not things to drag into the parlor. But the boys edged over toward the basket, eager to give out their gifts. Hans had bought three identical little figures of the Christ Child in the Manger for Mother and Thea and Tulla, and Anders distributed the results of a year's manual training at school—a birdhouse, a shelf, and a green-painted stool. They were actually not bad, considering that Anders had made them. That boy usually was remarkably clumsy with his hands.

On the table stood the large copper bowl full of nuts and fruits and cookies—samples of all the seven different kinds that the people of Gudbrandsdal think they must bake for Christmas. And Mother poured mead into the old glasses. No one liked the sweet, sticky mead, but Christmas would not be really Christmas without it. At least it made the children sleepy. Tulla yawned as if she meant to swallow her entire family, and she followed meek as a lamb when Thea came to take her upstairs to bed. Hans curled up on the sofa and took a cat nap. Only Anders and Mother remained sitting by the fire, looking at the Christmas tree, where candle after candle burned down into its holder and went out and gave off the sweet, warm odor of melted wax and spruce fir. The fire on the hearth had sunk into red coals that crackled and softly sighed. Mother and Anders had always liked so much to sit together, without talking.

At ten o'clock came the car. It was always Böe himself who drove them to Midnight Mass. He said he was glad to take that job Christmas Eve for his parents lived down at Hamar, so while Mother and the boys were at church he could slip in and wish them a Merry Christmas.

Saint Thorfin's Chapel at Hamar was only one large room in the Sisters' Hospital. But tonight it beamed with light and flowers, and at the left of the main altar the Manger was set up—everyone from Hamar was certain that their Manger was the most beautiful Manger in all Norway, if not in all Christendom. Young fir trees filled the entire corner, making it a bit of a real Norwegian forest. Green moss and red whortleberry foliage formed the carpet that the Stable stood on and in this green moss blanket were planted white tulips and hyacinths and pink Christmas begonias. Every family in the parish had sent a flowering potted plant to the Manger for that night. The Stable was built of white birch logs and roofed with straw— Mother Fulgentia had used the excelsior in which the altar wines came packed, for Mother Fulgentia was clever that way. And in the light of the big star that hung over the roof of the Stable, the little figures of Mary and Joseph kneeling before the Manger, and the young and old shepherds and shepherdesses with their sheep and lambs that they were bringing to Mary, looked exactly as if they were real.

"He *is* real," said little Aagot Larsen, who was kneeling beside Hans.

"Who is?" Hans whispered back, raptly interested.

"Jesus, of course. I saw him move his foot a little just now."

"Yes, but did you see the ox shake his head?" Hans asked.

"Yes. Oh dear, just so he does not get mad and gore the Virgin Mary!"

"He doesn't dare."

Mother and Mrs. Larsen started to shush their children, but on the bench in front, where the nuns were kneeling, Mother Fulgentia turned around, a finger on her lips. She smiled a smile so bright that her eyes vied with all the Christmas candles, and the children smiled back at her and ceased their whispering.

But when Mass was finished, and while all those of the parish who had a long way to go were served tea in the sister's parlor, Aagot and Hans outdid themselves telling each other all they had seen take place while Monseigneur said Mass. The Virgin Mary had spread the blanket over the child Jesus, but he had kicked it off again; the shepherds' dogs had come up and sniffed around and Saint Joseph had patted them. . . .

Perhaps the children imagined they had really seen the figures at the Manger move, as the lights and shadows thrown by the altar candles flickered and flamed across them. And they were encouraged to tell more and more, for the sisters seemed to have a great desire to laugh and to draw them out, though it is against the rules of the order to talk in the period between evening prayer and the morning Mass. Sister Rogata made so many curious signs and gestures to them that the youngsters had to go over to her and throw themselves into her lap a little while. Sister Rogata was every child's very special friend.

"It is because she has nothing to do with the school," Mother Fulgentia observed dryly.

Sister Rogata was the surgical nurse at the eye clinic.
It was two o'clock before Mother and the boys got
away and out to where Böe was waiting with the car.
And, miracle of miracles, the footpath was white, the
housetops white, and the tree branches etched in fine
white lines. The fall of snow was still so light that every
track was left blackly showing on the ground. But it
was *good* snow, a dense fall of hard, dry crystals. It beat
against the windshield with a light, prickling sound
when they began to drive.

The streets of Hamar lay deserted and still. And
when they got out of town, the road ran in the light of
the headlights like a white band through the forest's
black and white masses. Fences, gates, trees, and slum-
bering little houses slipped past. One of the best things
about this Christmas night drive, the boys felt, was to
know that they were up, and out driving, while everyone, for miles around their lake, was sound asleep!

Suddenly a bull moose started out of the forest near
Veldre. For some distance it ran ahead of them, with
nearly every hair of its gray-brown coat and every tip
of its antlers showing in the lights of the car. But when
Mother turned around to tell the boys to look, they lay
like rocks in the back seat, sound asleep, both of them.

The driving snow that had whirled furiously in
front of the windshield now turned into large feathery

flakes, tumbling down more and more thickly. Thea stood at the gate and had everything open as they drove up. The dogs knew Böe's car by its sound and always gave notice of its coming long before the car could be seen down the road. Now they stormed down to meet it, barking to high heaven, rolling in all the white, and lapping at it with their tongues.

The sleep-drugged boys tumbled out and saw that now it was really Christmas in Norway. . . .

That was why it was doubly festive to come to the table that stood there laden with all the very best Christmas things. It was hard to say whether this meal should be called supper or breakfast, but in communities where people keep up the old customs, they take the first bite of the Christmas pig and all the other meats sometime between midnight and daybreak of Christmas Day. That was why Thea had set out the headcheese and the mutton ham, the smoked reindeer tongue and the liver pudding. Hans, who was never allowed to drink coffee, got a cup tonight, and three drops of aquavit in a glass, so that he too could drink a toast and wish Merry Christmas once again.

Njord and Neri were wide awake, and Njord sat on his hind legs begging all the time that Mother ate. Neri lay in Anders's lap, and every once in a while he snatched a bite from the boy's plate. Of course only terribly spoiled dogs do such things, but these dogs were, unfortunately, just that. Besides, Christmas night they were allowed to do many things that were unacceptable for everyday.

Only Tulla was not down. It was better for her to sleep undisturbed. Tomorrow, when the others were in bed, Tulla would sit by the window where she never tired of looking at the big flag that hung outside, furling and unfurling, and then falling against the flagpole again—to billow out and show the blue and white cross upon the scarlet field—and then come back to hide itself like some living thing. . . . Even when the air was still, or when it was snowing and the flag hung limp, Tulla sat waiting faithfully, staring. . . .

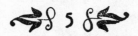

IT IS THE CUSTOM IN NORWAY THAT ON CHRISTMAS DAY
people stay quietly at home, or go out only to be with
their closest relatives. Even the skiers who swarmed
over all the roads and fields, beaming with delight over
the first snow of the year, kept together in family
groups. Big boys, who ordinarily spend all their free
time on their ski club's training ground, stay home and
take a quiet morning walk with their mamma, and
sometimes with grandmamma too. Fathers putter
around in the fields this day instead of going to their
cottages in the mountains. They have their tiniest
youngster with them, a boy or girl of two or three, who
got his, or her, first pair of skis under the Christmas
tree this year and today has them on for the first time.

But Anders came home to the late dinner, cheeks
red and hair damp, and with eyes that were dark and
shining. The whole boy seemed to be aglow. He had
been clear up to Nordseter.

"Three hours up, and half an hour down, and as soft as velvet, mother!"

Then Mother knew that from now on until the last snow in the mountains became unusable sometime in the spring, Anders would think of little else than skiing. All his free time would be used for practicing, and every Sunday morning he would disappear with a truckload of boys bound for some ski contest to the north, or south, or east, or west. Anders had not yet reached high on the prize list. He was too thin and light, even in his own age group. But the judges said he had fine style, and he worked hard, so he would be good in time, when he had taken on some weight. Skiing interfered with his schoolwork, of course. But Mother had the same weakness as most Norwegian mothers. It was unfortunate if his marks were altogether too poor, but if the boy could keep it up until he became an outstanding skier, she would be dreadfully proud. Secretly she pasted into a scrapbook all the little newspaper clippings in which Anders's name appeared, even though it was only one of the lowest prizes he had won.

Hans had not one particle of such vanity. He went on long trips with Magne or Ole Henrik, his friends, equipped with much good food in their knapsacks. Up in the forest and on the ridges were little farms where they could buy coffee and ginger ale, before they skied down. But to ski "just to have people standing around gaping on the hill, gape at me, that's just dumb," said Hans.

On Second Christmas Day everyone in the house had to get up early, for today the guests from Oslo were arriving on the noon train. And although Mother and Thea had been working for many days to get ready for them, there were many things to arrange at the last minute.

Böe brought two cars. Mother took Tulla with her in one, for Grandmother was always so happy when Tulla came to meet her. Anders and Hans went in the other car, and in the course of the journey to the station they managed to become furious enemies. Anders had a bad habit of bossing his brother, and Hans did not like to be bossed by anyone. This time it was Brit they had quarreled about.

"Anders does not have to tell me I must not tease Brit! I guess I am just as much her uncle as he is!"

It was still snowing hard and the place outside the station was almost impenetrable, it was so filled with buses and cars from the many hotels and sanatoriums in and around town, and with horses and sleighs from the farms. The station platform swarmed with people. Half the town was there to meet Christmas guests, and the other half whose guests had arrived Christmas Eve was down to see who was coming on the train. The hotels were almost full and still more people were expected. Many Danes always came up here at Christmastime to ski—and one could tell the Danes half a mile away as large parties of them came driving down Main Street. They talked so loud and shouted and laughed; besides, they were always clad in all the colors of the rainbow— red and blue and yellow trousers and striped and flowered jerseys. But they were astonishingly good skiers, many of them, and those who were not good were at least daring and rolled down the slopes blithely.

The train was more than an hour late, the station-master announced. Special trains, overcrowding, and obstacles caused by the snow along the line had made chaos of the traffic, but that too was part of Christmas. There was much jollity at the station on these occasions. Mother greeted acquaintances from Oslo and acquaintances from town, and everyone had to wish everyone else Merry Christmas and agree to meet sometime during the holidays. Anders and Hans forgot to quarrel and planned skiing trips with their friends and made dates with the girls for the ball at the Bank Second New Year's Day. And the snow fell faster and faster. Soon everyone looked like a snowman or a witch, and inside the railroad station restaurant the floor and tables floated in half-melted snow. People came in to pass the time over a cup of coffee and then dashed out to peer down the tracks for the train.

They neither saw nor heard it in the falling snow until it was almost upon them. Anders and Hans burrowed a way for themselves through the mass of people in order to be the first to greet Grandmother. There she stood in the window, waving, when suddenly Anders discovered Neri between his legs. And in the middle of a great snow flurry, Njord and the beagle from Victoria Hotel were engaged in savage combat. Mother and the hotel boy threw themselves upon the dogs to separate them. How it ever happened that the dogs had got out and followed them clear down to the station it was hard to say. But when Anders and Mother finally got them into the car, Hans, proud as a peacock, was already escorting the Christmas guests. It had been he, after all, who had had to find them in that crowd on the platform and show them the way to Böe's cars.

Now followed a good deal of discussion about who should sit with whom. Hans wanted to sit beside Grandmother, in the car where Mother and Tulla were, but he wanted Brit beside him also. He became annoyed with Anders again, for Anders without any more ado had lifted Brit up in his arms and whisked her into the other car. Anders, naturally, was going to sit beside Gunhild, their half sister, for she and Anders had always been the best of friends. Böe and Godfather and Aunt Signe were busy getting all the baggage arranged and all the skis tied fast on the outside of the car. Today, skis and ski poles bristled from everything on wheels. The girls—Aunt Signe's three, and Ulla from Stockholm—tumbled in and out of the two cars and did not know where they wanted to sit or where there would be room for them. The twins, Siri-Kari and Anne-Lotte, looked pale, for they always got trainsick.

Finally the whole party was disposed of, one way or another, and Böe started off. It was almost dinnertime when they got home, but Thea had nevertheless laid the tea table in the large parlor, for Grandmother always had to have tea the moment she arrived. Thea would certainly postpone dinner an hour, for she knew everyone had to speak with everyone else and there was such a lot to talk about. The children hoped that the rest of the Christmas presents would be distributed at once, but Mother said no to that idea.

"That will have to wait," she said. "There are so many of us that it will take too much time!"

It was a whole year since all the family had been together. Grandmother had been here in the summer, and the girls from Oslo had come up rather often, whenever they had a few days' vacation, but Mother's sister, Aunt Signe, and her husband, whom the children called Godfather because he was godfather to Anders, had not been here since last Christmas. And Ulla from Stockholm, the daughter of Mother's other sister who was married in Sweden, was traveling alone for the first time in her life. Since she was Hans's age, seven years old, it was rather impressive, for Hans had never been allowed to travel alone even so far as Oslo. Grandmother was still rather shocked over the fact that Ulla's mother had dared to let her go so far alone— but she was beaming at the same time for now she had all her grandchildren, except Ulla's little brother, gathered round her.

Gunhild had not been here since Brit was a tiny tot who could hardly stand. Now she was over two, and could both run and talk all she needed—and a little more besides. Both Anders and Hans thought it a frightful lot of fun that they were uncles and they admired their niece tremendously! To think that Brit was not in the least afraid of the two black dogs that looked so wild and were carrying on so! For Njord seemed to think he must show Grandmother how delighted he was to see her by nearly knocking her down. And all these strange children he had to bark at, so that they would have the proper respect for him, for it would be too much of a good thing if they all petted and hugged him until he had no peace! Neri flew around like the little fool he was, trying to do everything Njord did. Finally Brit got both her fists entwined in Njord's fur, where she held on until Njord positively had to shake her loose. After that he went and lay down under Mother's writing table in the other room and Neri took refuge in Mother's lap.

The cats did not make an appearance at all when there were so many strangers in the house. They lay in Thea's bed, when they were not in the kitchen, eating, or out walking in the snow.

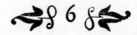

THEA HAD DECORATED THE LONG BREAKFAST TABLE with sprigs of evergreen, candles, and flowers. It sagged under all the good Christmas food. And in the snow outside the door stood the bottles of beer, and the old brandy decanter from Great-grandfather's house. God-father was very particular that the Christmas brandy should be the temperature of the snow.

As they sat waiting for Thea to come down with Tulla, and Gunhild to come with Brit, the children ate cookies and cracked nuts, for all during the Christmas season the big old copper bowl filled with fruit and nuts and cookies stood on a table in the corner.

A telephone call for Anders. . . . Soon he was back in the room with a rush.

"Mother, would you please pack my knapsack? I must have enough food along for twenty-four hours at least. That was from Nordseter Hotel . . . two Danes went out as it was getting dark last night, and they haven't come back. Now they are asking some of the

45

Boy Scouts to come along and look for them. It was foggy and snowing in the mountains yesterday, of course. Just like Danes to do some fool thing like that."

Grandmother was about to protest, for Grandmother was Danish, but Anders waved her aside:

". . . talk about it when I get home, grandmother. But, say, grandmother, lend me your pocket flashlight, will you? Both batteries are burned out in mine."

Again Grandmother started to protest. She could not give up her flashlight! Every time she woke up at night she wanted to see what time it was.

"Mother will give you a candle and some matches, grandmother. I *must* have a pocket flashlight with me."

So Grandmother went to fetch her precious flashlight.

"And you, mother, you must lend me both thermos bottles for coffee, and I ought to have a little aquavit along too, just in case we find them. But hurry up, then! The car may be here any second."

Anders stood ready, skis and all, as the truck stopped before the gate. Mother followed him out. It was rather comforting to see that all the other boys in the car were older than Anders—several of them were young men.

"Well, I know you are used to the mountains, Anders. I can depend on you to be careful and not get separated from your party."

For now the snow was tumbling down again so thickly one could not see more than a few ski lengths ahead.

"Yes. Yes, mamma."

When Anders considered any remark of Mother's ill-timed he called her "mamma."

"Don't worry about me. . . . Of course you realize I probably won't be home tonight. . . . Yes, certainly, I'll ask the hotel to give you a ring the minute they find those Danes. By the way, the mother of one of them is on the way down to see you," Anders remembered suddenly. "They asked me to tell you. It's someone you know—she's a writer, I think they said."

"Do you know her name? Didn't they say?"

"Yes, but I can't remember it. 'Swan,' I think maybe. Or maybe 'Baer.' *Some* kind of animal anyway. Well, take care of yourselves."

Indoors, the family was still waiting for breakfast and Aunt Signe was trying to soothe the ruffled tempers. Grandmother was annoyed, for she considered Anders altogether too young to be going on a searching party; besides, why must people always pick on the Danes? Godfather was saying he did not always pick on the Danes, but they annoyed him—yes, and all the other foreigners, as well, who staged these disappearing acts in the mountain resorts every blessed winter. Why couldn't they listen to the guides who tried to make it clear to them that when there was a heavy fog, or when it was snowing, it was no time to go skiing? For then searching parties had to be made up, lumbermen and farmers had to leave their work, often for days at a time, for sometimes it took days to find a couple of lost tourists in such terrain as the mountains hereabouts, with mile upon mile of little hills and valleys running hither and thither. There ought to be notices posted at every resort that tourists who got lost must pay the searchers for the time spent looking for them. Maybe that would put an end to the nuisance. But that would probably never be done.

It has been the rule in Norway for hundreds of years that, when anyone gets lost in the forests or on the mountains, all the men in the neighborhood go out and search for him until he is found, dead or alive. When it was one of the country people who got lost it was usually someone out on a necessary errand—someone going to or from a saeter, or crossing the mountain into the neighboring valley, or someone out hunting or fishing, not persons out for fun. Just because tourists who did not know any better abused good old customs, people, at least in this part of the country, had no desire to change any of them.

Mother had just managed to snatch a bite of break-fast when Thea came in.

"There is a lady asking to see Madam. Shall I show her into the parlor?"

The moment Mother opened the parlor door, a big yellow-haired woman in orange-colored sports clothes sprang into her arms. The woman's face was so red and swollen from tears that one could scarcely tell what she looked like, and she sobbed and sobbed.

Mother tried to console her.

"They'll find them. They *always* do. And it was not cold last night, and there are so many cabins and saeters in the mountains, perhaps they got indoors somewhere last night! Ah, it could have been much, much worse."

The ice was still undependable in many places on the lakes up there, and in such weather it was impossible to see far ahead. But this Mother did not say. She comforted the woman as well as she could. She had realized that this was a Mrs. Jytte Hjorth, whom she had met at some congress in Copenhagen.

Mrs. Hjorth's son had just been graduated from medical school; he had passed his examination brilliantly, but he felt rather tired afterward, and so Mrs. Hjorth had come up here with him so that her Egil could have a rest. . . . And yesterday afternoon he had gone skiing with a friend. . . .

She cried and cried. Mrs. Hjorth was a widow and her son was her only child.

Mother got the fire lit in the fireplace and settled Mrs. Hjorth in a comfortable chair before its warmth. Coffee and a dainty breakfast tray helped to calm the poor woman. She had been so upset she had not tasted food since yesterday afternoon. Aunt Signe called the hotel every half hour, but there was no news about Dr. Hjorth and his companion. However, in the mountains it was almost clear now and was beginning to freeze. That would lighten the work of the rescuers a great deal. The fog had sunk down into the valley. Here the weather was gray and gloomy, and in spite of the candles the parlor was dark.

At dinnertime Mrs. Hjorth decided she *must* go up to the hotel again. She could not endure sitting here any longer. And she did so want Mother to come along.

Mother was not entirely unwilling. She was a little uneasy about Anders. . . . All the youngsters set up a vast howl of protest when she told them.

But, they protested, the Third Christmas Day, the very first whole day they were all together, was the best day in the whole year, with an extra special dinner and with dancing around the lighted Christmas tree afterward, and everything! And then. in Mother's big bedroom, after they had all undressed, they would run around and play in their nightgowns and pajamas, until Mother came up and lit the candles in front of that lovely little crib Hans had! And told stories! Now if she and Anders were both going to be away, the whole day would be spoiled.

Aunt Signe promised that Thea and she would do the best they could for the children. Besides, they had Grandmother, Mother reminded them. All the children idolized their grandmother. She was so tiny and so dainty, with her snow-white hair and her delicate little face. Because she never petted them, but talked with them as if they were as grown-up and as clever as she herself, each of the boys and girls was certain that he, or she, was Grandmother's very own favorite.

Yes, that was true, Grandmother was there; that would make things as good as possible until Mother got back.

It was not cheerful at the little mountain hotel. All the men guests were, of course, out on the searching party. Sitting around in the lobbies and parlors, the women were knitting or trying to read, or playing solitaire, but they were restless. Over and over, they asked Mr. Nesheim, the owner, the same questions.

"It would not surprise me," Mr. Nesheim declared, "if we have to get out and look for some of the searchers, as soon as we have hauled in the Danes!"

Mother sat up all night with Mrs. Hjorth, sleeping when Mrs. Hjorth slept, listening when Mrs. Hjorth was not sleeping. Betweentimes, she speculated upon where Anders was that night, and how things were with him.

At nine Mr. Nesheim awakened them.

"Well, Mrs. Hjorth, now you can be happy. Your son will be here in a few hours. They found them at the southern end of Kroksjoen. Dr. Hjorth is all right, but the lawyer, Petersen, has hurt his foot, so he will have to be brought down by ski sled. By the by," he said to Mother, as he answered Mrs. Hjorth's thousand and one questions, "Anders is down in the dining room now."

Anders looked up from the platter of bacon and eggs —much too obviously casual and uninterested.

"For heaven's sake, mother, are you here? Ah, you've been sitting up with that Danish lady, haven't you? No, I'm not in the least tired. . . . We hunted down through that draw along Deep Water Creek, you know —and all around Deep Water Lake. We went to every cabin and every saeter, you see. Finally we turned in at Ramstad's cabin—Nils and I had been sent out with two others from the hotel here, you see—a Dane, a good fellow, by the way, good on skis—and a Swede. We finally convinced them it was no use wandering around in the mountains after it had got pitch-dark, so we turned in. . . . Lay down to sleep a bit, planning to start hunting down toward Hynna as soon as it got light. But then Aasen came early this morning and said they had found them. It was Aasen's party that found them, you see."

Suddenly the boy lost his mask of indifference.

"And, mother, do you know what? Nils and I got to go along with Aasen—Johan Aasen, you know—from the Ramstad cabin clear up to the peak above Clear Water. Out on the ice he left us, of course, but we had managed to keep up with him clear to there! Mother, you can't imagine what a swell fellow he is—Aasen—"

Johan Aasen, the lumberjack from Lismarka, champion skier and prize winner at ever so many ski tournaments both at home and abroad, was the idol and hero of all the boys. The two Boy Scouts who had been on this journey with him over the mountain obviously thought the expedition in search of the vanished Danes just a lucky adventure.

"Aasen said, by the way, that the doctor—the one who is the son of that friend of yours—is a smart fellow. When he saw they were lost, he said they should burrow down in the snow and stay there until daylight. But then the lawyer went to fetch some water—they could hear a stream running nearby under the snow where they were lying—and he stepped down between two rocks and broke his ankle. . . . Tired? Who, me? Of course not, why should I be tired?"

But just the same Anders was quite willing to drive home with Mother in the car "—if Nils wants to, that is. Otherwise, we'll ski."

But Nils also was glad to ride. They were standing out on the *tun*, the three of them, and the boys were tying their skis to the car, when a man on skis streaked past—a slim young man, light-haired, brown-skinned, with sharp light-blue eyes.

"Thanks for your company." His voice was low and gentle. He nodded to the boys.

"Same to you!" Anders turned to his mother. "*That* was Johan Aasen." His whole face beamed.

Nils got in front with the chauffeur, and Anders crawled in with Mother in the back seat. They had scarcely started to drive, before Anders began to sway toward Mother's breast. He slept. Mother peeped at Nils, but Nils too was slumped down, his head nodding, nodding. . . .

"Tired." The chauffeur grinned.

So Mother put her arm around her big boy, so that his head should rest well against her shoulder, and sound asleep, the two Boy Scouts drove home from their first lifesaving expedition into the mountains.

AFTER THAT THE CHRISTMAS HOLIDAYS PASSED
quickly with an abundance of fun and good things
all around—except quiet and order in the house.

Every morning there was the same Jerusalem disturbance. It took time to get that herd of children to
the breakfast table. And afterward, it took still more
time to get them rigged out in their coats and caps and
steered out the door. It was necessary to search out the
least wet of their garments from all the things that were
drying all over the house. And someone was always sit-
ing down to crack nuts and nibble at a cooky instead of
lacing his, or her, boots, or changing from indoor
clothes into ski clothes. Then there would be scolding
and fussing.

"Worse youngsters than you I think could not be
found if one searched the whole world round—until
one got back here again," Thea stormed.

All the grownups were tired and cross—though in

good humor at heart—when at long last the flock was ready to be driven out into the snow.

On the slope between the house and the kitchen garden, Anders had made a fine ski course that was just right for little children to practice on, and he had built two jumps, one tiny one and one a little higher. Some friends of Hans's and some friends the girls had made on a previous visit at Mother's, played on the hill all day long, coming to the kitchen door to ask for a drink of water—meaning pop and cookies!—every once in a while. Thea scolded, because they disturbed her in her dinner preparations, and Ingeborg, the maid, and Mari Moen, who came every day now to help Ingeborg with the ironing and the care of all the children's clothes, were surly and cross over all the trouble those youngsters made. But the children cared not one bit about the womenfolks' fussing—they got everything they wanted anyway.

Anders usually disappeared between meals. The other children were so much younger than he that he stayed elsewhere with his companions. Only when Brit was out rolling in the snow, herself a little white ball in her white kidskin coat, was he there to ski down the little "baby hill" with her in front of him standing on his skis. One day he dug out of the attic a pair of tiny skis that he himself had got when he was two years old. For a few hours he kept it up—wildly eager to teach his little niece to ski. He led her around and around down on the lawn, picking her up and brushing her off every time she fell, replacing her skis as fast as she lost them, and scolding severely, his face scowling, when Brit cried because she had snow up her sleeves.

"Shame, shame on you! I thought you were a fine little Norwegian girl, Bitta."

Next day he was entirely willing to let whosoever wished take over the task of teaching Brit to ski!

So then Hans and the girls had something to quarrel about.

"I think it would be a fine idea for you to remember she is my niece," Hans said, greatly annoyed. *"You* are not Brit's uncle, are you?"

"Uncle!" Siri-Kari and Anne-Lotte jeered in unison. "We'd have to be *aunts,* anyway! Wouldn't you like us to be your aunts, Brit?"

"Poor little Aunt Tulla," said Brit mournfully, shaking her head. Her mother had taught her to say that when she patted Tulla good night and good morning.

"There, you see!" Hans cried triumphantly. "Brit knows very well that only Tulla is her aunt."

Little as she was, Brit was a finished coquette. She knew full well that Hans was miserable when she pretended she would rather have Siri-Kari and Anne-Lotte pull her around on her skis. But when Hans sought comfort in the company of Little Signe or Ulla, she ran away from the girls and came to him, demanding that he pay attention to her.

"You wouldn't come over and say good morning to this ugly man, would you, Brit?" Uncle Godfather said to her one morning. And now she shouted "Ugly Man, Ugly Man" at him every time she saw him. Grandmother was the only person for whom she had a little respect, for Grandmother had smacked her fingers one morning when Brit threw nutshells all over the floor and chairs and potted plants. Since then Brit sat very still when Grandmother looked sternly at her. But if Grandmother was reading or embroidering, Brit had to go over to her just the same. She would lay her hands in Grandmother's lap and make her voice as sweet as sugar:

"Brit's good girl now, grandma. Brit's so good, so-o-o good today."

For the one thing Brit absolutely could not stand was that anyone should not pay her full attention.

New Year's Eve all the children were allowed to sit up to see the new year in. The Christmas tree was lighted for the last time—tomorrow Mother would take off the trimmings, hang bits of fat and lumps of tallow on it and set it outside the door for the chickadees.

The youngest children—Little Signe and Ulla and Hans—had a hard time holding their eyes open when the clock approached ten. But then they all sat down around the long table in the dining room to play Black Peter. Whenever one of the grownups had to be Black Peter and got whiskers painted on with burnt cork, all the youngsters howled with delight. Anders had taken charge of the cork, and when it was Grandmother who had to have her face blackened, he drew, in place of the usual mustachios, some elegant beau-catcher curls down her cheeks.

"Grandmother, they're becoming!"

Grandmother had to go look at herself in the mirror and it was easy to see she agreed that she looked well with beau catchers.

"You look like one of Napoleon's generals," declared Anders.

"Napoleon," said Grandmother disgustedly, "was one of the most abominable individuals who ever destroyed life and happiness for worthy people by the ten thousands! I most certainly do not wish to look like one of his generals!"

"Of course not, grandmother. You look like a Danish poet of the Golden Age," consoled Mother.

Grandmother seemed to like that better.

And now the hands of the old grandfather clock in the corner said twelve and everyone took his glass of mulled red wine and went out under the open sky. The night was cold and clear with stars, and northern lights played high above, over the edge of the black ridge to the north of the valley.

The church clock downtown struck twelve, and the bells began to welcome the new year. Everyone wished everyone else Happy New Year, and thanked one another for the things of the old year.

"Yes, thanks for the old year!" Aunt Signe and Mother said and kissed Grandmother, and when the children saw that, they all wanted to kiss their mothers.

"Thanks, thanks for the old—"

On Second New Year's Day there was always a ball in the banquet hall of the Savings Bank—from five until nine for children, from nine on for the grownups. But Aunt Signe and Godfather took the little ones, for they enjoyed watching them dance.

Mother remained at home. Tulla still sat by the window—there had been so many birds in the Christmas sheaves today, and she could not understand why, now that it was dark, no more came; she was waiting for them to return. Mother sat down beside her and looked out at the garden sleeping under the deep snow, and

saw beyond the snow-laden trees the twinkling lights
of the town. Mother had her arm around Tulla when
she noticed the new moon, hanging thin as a splinter
and pale gold over the edge of the ridge to the south.
God be praised, thought Mother, and drew Tulla still
closer to her side—for it is an old belief in Norway that
what one holds in one's hands when one sees the New
Year's new moon, one shall not lose that year.

Anders came down just then. He was wearing his
new sailor suit for the first time. A sailor suit is the
only conceivable "dress-up" suit for boys in Norway.
Mother took his hand and held it as she looked at the
moon.

"You're getting so big, boy, that when that suit is
worn out I suppose I'll have to get you a tuxedo for
parties."

Anders laughed, a little embarrassed.

"I'll sit here with you and Tulla awhile, mother. It
is no fun for us older ones to go so early. Can't even
dance, with the floor crawling with little trolls."

Mother remembered very well from other years—the
older children were fish out of water at the New Year's
Ball. They did not feel like mixing with the little ones,
who were romping around playing their games right
among the dancers. They longed to stay on into the
evening and dance when the grownups danced—and

the grownups were not very enthusiastic about having them there too long.

But it was a mere transition, as the fox observed when he was being skinned.

Tulla was going to get her sleigh ride after all. True, it could not be in the evening, but she had seen the Christmas lights in Main Street many times anyway, for as often as Mother or Thea had to go downtown on errands, Tulla had been allowed to go along in the car.

Epiphany, or Twelfth Day, marks the end of Christmas in Norway. *Hellig Tre Kongers Dag*—Holy Three Kings Day—it is called. In olden days it was called Saint Knut's Day, so people said, "Saint Knut drives Christmas away." That was why it was the custom in many places in the country for people that day to leave their farms and homes to go driving and racing on the roads and on the ice-covered lakes. They called it the Christmas Race. And they believed the trolls raced that night, led by a terrible old hag of a troll who was called Kari-Tretten, or Kari the Thirteenth.

This year all Mother's guests were going on a Christmas race and the other children teased Siri-Kari about her name. Was she Kari the Thirteenth? Kari the Thirteenth, Kari the Thirteenth . . .

"All right, go right ahead and call me that," said

Siri-Kari patronizingly. "I don't care, because then I'll be the one to ride in the first sleigh."

But as the five sleighs drew up, one behind the other, in front of the gate, it appeared that Mother wished to ride in the first sleigh, for that was where Tulla sat. Petter himself always drove the first sleigh, and Petter had been Tulla's driver every Christmas. . . . He had the same horses he had last year, too—Rauen and Maja. All the children knew them and had to go down and give them bread crusts and sugar lumps, before the procession started.

Tulla sat between Mother and Thea, so they could support her when they went around the curves. She was bundled up to her nose, and the bearskin rug was pulled well up around her. On the seat opposite sat Gunhild with Brit—Mother wished to keep an eye on them because Gunhild was rather timid about driving with horses, even though she thought it was great fun too. But what if she should get so frightened, at some sharp turn or other, that she should let Brit fall out in the snowdrift. . . .

The other children were naturally even more unaccustomed to sleigh riding. They were all children of the automobile age. Ulla from Stockholm had actually never been in a sleigh before.

"Oh, *dear* Aunt Sigrid, may I sit by the chauffeur?"

Petter chuckled and helped her up beside him on the coachman's seat. And so she called him "uncle," for Swedish children say uncle or aunt to all grownups.

"Why does Uncle have a fishing pole along?" asked Ulla, pointing in astonishment at Petter's whip.

The children had been permitted to invite as many of their friends as there was room for in the sleighs. The last sleigh was only an old freight sled. The youngsters sat on boards and sacks of hay, and it was unbelievable the number there was room for that way.

It was rather cold, but the sky was brilliantly blue and the sun was shining and made the snow-clad trees and the wide moors glitter as if with diamonds, and ruts in the road and the fences and trees threw blue shadows across the snow. Up on the ridge the snow lay so deep over the forest that it looked like one goldenly white mass in the sunlight—"exactly as if it were all covered with whipped cream," Hans observed materialistically.

The sleigh bells rang silvery clear and melodious as the five sleighs began to move. Down through Main Street they went, the children shouting and waving to everyone they knew and people waving back and laughing at the procession.

As they got out of town the horses were really given their heads. The music of the sleigh bells rang still louder and more happily, steam rose from the horses like thin white smoke, and the warm, living smell of them drifted back to the people in the sleighs.

Up on the ridge Petter left the main road and took a little road that went through the forest to the Gjorlia farm. Apparently no one had been over it since the snow came except someone logging. It was so narrow that snow from the drifts alongside fell into the sleigh, and from the branches that almost interlocked above the road, white cascades descended upon the passing sleighs. And it was bumpety bump, bumpety bump, the whole way. In most places it would have been impossible to overturn, so high lay the snow on either side. But in other places the road ran along the edge of the precipitous slope above Gjorlia Creek—and here Mother and Thea held Tulla tightly, for the sleigh tipped so to one side that it seemed nearly to overhang the creek bed. Gunhild turned quite pale and pulled Brit close. But Brit laughed, and Tulla laughed. They thought it only fun to be tossed here and there. And Petter was such a skillful driver, and Rauen and Maja were so steady and dependable. But the freight sled behind would *surely* overturn—or at least two or three youngsters would roll out, thought Mother, rather un easily—though, even if they did, they could not possi bly get hurt in the deep snow.

But when they had got to the bottom of all the hills and were out on the road beside the lake, it became apparent that the trip had been made without the slightest mishap. Despite the fact that one of the horses they were using on the sled in which Grandmother and Aunt Signe sat, was a quite young and rather lively little mare.

It was on the way home, in Main Street, that Hans fell out of the freight sled. The flock of youngsters had gradually become quite wild, swatting and tickling one another and howling to high heaven—when suddenly Hans went kerplunk into the street, under the very feet of the horses of the sleigh behind.

It is true enough that a horse almost never steps on any living thing. Even a horse in full gallop is incredibly alert in this matter and manages to stop short or otherwise avoid stepping on anything that moves. It is only with inexperienced and high-strung horses that there is ever an accident.

But that young gray mare, Gurli, met the situation as if she were the staidest old horse in the world. All went well. Later Hans was downright proud because he alone, out of the entire party, had fallen out of the sleigh.

That evening on the dinner table were the three-pronged candles in honor of *Hellig Tre Kongers Dag*.

It was the last dinner at which they would all be together—for this time. Gunhild and Brit had to leave that night, for tomorrow her husband's boat would arrive. And Godfather and Aunt Signe were to leave next day, for the children had to get back to school.

But next morning as Aunt Signe was packing their bags and the cousins were outside skiing down the little hill a few more times just to say good-by, Anne-Lotte fell and wrenched her ankle. Kind Dr. Konow came up, felt her foot and said the best thing would be for her to stay off it completely a few days. She ought perhaps to stay here with her aunt for a while.

So Anne-Lotte lay on the sofa in the dining room, and on a table beside her she had chocolate with whipped cream, and cookies, and fruit that Thea had given her "for consolation." Siri-Kari, Little Signe, and Ulla were more than a little envious of her as they bade her farewell. She would get out of school for one whole week more, and they knew that both Mother and Thea would spoil her with good things and amusing books and everything else they could think of to make her "sickness" a pleasant extra vacation.

That same afternoon Mrs. Jytte Hjorth called to say good-by. And she wanted so to say good-by to Anders too.

"The delightful boy," she cried, rushing toward him

as he came in and bowed his best dancing-school bow. Then she took his face between both her hands and gave him a resounding kiss on both cheeks. The poor boy's face became as red as beetroot and he looked as if he did not know what to do with himself in his embarrassment.

"Here is a little something as a remembrance of the time you helped save my son's life," the lady said, thrusting a little package into his hand.

"Nobody saved Dr. Hjorth's life!" Anders protested, visibly annoyed. "The doctor would have managed all right, even if no one had gone out looking for them. It was only that they were so dumb as to go out in bad weather. Otherwise the doctor was a smart fellow. He would have found his way out as soon as the weather cleared up."

But then he realized what Mother meant by her winking and blinking at him and by all the weird faces she was making.

"Well, thank you a thousand times, Mrs. Hjorth. I just think it's too much, that's all. Oh, that's wonderful! Oh, yes, yes, of course. Oh, you can be sure I am glad to have *that*!"

It was a fine fountain pen.

"I just think there's no sense in it," Anders said when the woman had left. "I didn't do anything. If she had given us a present for the Boy Scout lodge there'd be more sense to it. There were five men from the lodge out looking. . . .

"It cost eighteen crowns at Stribold, mother," he said, investigating, and full of admiration. "But you may have it for ten, mother, if you will buy it from me. Then I can give the money to our treasury."

"Or you could give the fountain pen to the bazaar. You are going to have a bazaar next month," Mother suggested.

"But if you buy it from me you won't have to worry any more about what to give me for my birthday."

Mother had to laugh.

"My boy, I think you are getting practical!"

"Practical? Say, if there is anything I am, it is a practical man.— Ouch, let go my hair!"

He pretended to cry and wriggled his head away from under Mother's hand.

"First that Danish friend of yours pounces on me and kisses me, and then my very own mother tries to scalp me."

PART II

THE SEVENTEENTH OF MAY

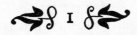

I

"WINTER-SPRING" IS THE NAME PEOPLE IN NORWAY give to that odd season that begins in February. When day after day the sun beams down from a high and cloudless deep-blue sky and every morning the whole world is encrusted with glistening frost crystals—but later in the day all the eaves are dripping. The sun licks the snow from the trees, and one sees the tops of the birches beginning to turn a shiny brown and the bark of the aspens taking on the greenish tinge that betokens spring.

Snowdrifts still lie high along the roads and fences and on the fields the snowcrust shines like silver in the sun, the ski tracks drawing bright lines in crisscross. Crows and magpies fly about with twigs in their bills. They have more or less begun to repair last year's nests, and once in a while they pierce the stillness of the winter day with their squawks and chatter.

As soon as the sun goes down there is biting cold. But a reflection of the daylight remains, a fringe of flame, along the black-forested ridge to the southwest. For many hours afterward a light, the color of old green glass, lingers on the horizon. In the morning long icicles hang from all the eaves, but in the course of the forenoon shining drops begin to fall. And every day is a little longer and little lighter than the day before.

It is a glorious time of year for the children and the young people.

The boys came home from school and bolted their food—they were going over on the hill for ski training. And they did not come home until the first stars began to twinkle in the sky. After the evening meal there was coasting on the long roadways that wind with many a hairpin curve down from the mountain and straight across the town. These roads were far from safe for coasting. There was a great deal of traffic on them—cars and buses and trucks—and moreover they cut across Main Street, which also is the main road leading into the valley. Mothers could do nothing but warn: "Now do be careful!" And the sons pointed out that they certainly did not need to be told that! No one would go coasting and get killed for the fun of it.

When and how those same boys ever studied their lessons and wrote their exercises was hard to conceive.

But they must have done so, somehow or other, for their grades at school were no lower than for the fall semester. Perhaps the teachers were more lenient at ski time. Every school had a ski tournament during the winter, and in place of physical training courses the boys were allowed to go with the physical training teacher on skiing trips up through the forest. And it was possible to "glance" at the lessons in the morning, before one had to start, for on skis or Swedish "kick-sled" it took only five minutes to get to school. So the boys did not leave home until after they really should have been at their desks.

"Kick-sledding" is a Swedish invention, but it had become tremendously popular in Norway in the course of a few years. It sounded disrespectful when Anders offered to kick Mother downtown, if she had some errands to do, and strange when Thea kicked Tulla a long way out in the sun every morning. Thea sought vainly to get her to keep her sunglasses on—Tulla took them off every time she saw her chance and slung them in the snow at the roadside.

There was always some accident or other. Little by little the ski courses and skiing roads became worn down to bare ice. It hurt to fall now. In homes all about the countryside were boys lying abed who had fallen and had water on the knee or a slight concussion of the brain. It was only strange that no one got seriously hurt more frequently. On those hills owned by the various ski clubs, where the real training took place, fresh snow was, of course, hauled in, and the snow on the slope below the jump was kept from getting packed and hard. But the slopes in the forests were frightful; many of them were being used for logging. Yet just when they were about to become impossible, a few days' snowfall usually came and saved the situation—and all the courses were velvet again.

It was an enjoyable time for the grownups as well. The sun grew stronger day by day, and the potted plants in the windows had their own springtime. The Norwegians console themselves for the length of their winter with splendid window gardens. The rooms were fragrant with the odor of sprouting bulbs and tulips. The day it was possible to eat dinner without turning on the lights was always a red-letter day—even though one did have to turn them on the day following, if there was fish for dinner.

March is always colder than February, with frequent dark and foggy days, and occasionally a howling snow-storm that lasts from three to four days. But "March is not so bad, for she makes half the road bare," the old saying goes and it always holds true. A strip of black earth grins up from the southerly edge of the road without fail before the month of March has ended.

Every day Hans came home at least an hour late for dinner, soaking wet from his leather boots to his hair and streaked with horse manure. He and his playmates could never resist the temptation to make canals of the ruts that were overflowing with water everywhere in the middle of the day. They built dams in them and measured the depth of the water by stepping into it!

"Now you must not go out on the Holme pond, Hans," said Mother sternly. Hans stood, music case in hand, ready to leave for his music lesson. "Do you hear?"

"Oh, no, I won't ever do that again," Hans peered sorrowfully up at his mother. "Not after seeing that poor girl who tried to slide on the ice there. She plunked in, poor thing . . ." Hans heaved a sigh that seemed to come from the depths of his soul.

"What? What happened to her?"

"Oh, she's lying there on the bottom yet, I suppose," said Hans in a sepulchral voice. "She never came up again. Oh, she yelled so, mother. I'll never forget it as long as I live. It was the last time I went to Mrs. Anker's. That was when I saw it."

"But to think you didn't try—" began Mother, completely horrified. Then she continued rather more calmly. "How did it happen that you did not go out

77

and save her? The Holme pond is no deeper than your waist anywhere. Hans, Hans, you simply must not run around and tell such stories! That's lying, Hans!"

"Is it?" asked Hans, surprised. "I thought lying was when I lied when you asked if I've done something I've done that is naughty to do."

"Yes, of course—that is the worst kind of lie. But it is also lying when you go around telling something you have made up, so that people think it is true."

"Is it?" asked Hans again. "But, mother, then you lie too, when you tell us about the time you and Aunt Ragnhild and Aunt Signe were young?"

"I most certainly do not, Hans. I do not tell anything but what was really so."

"Is it *true* that you went by steamboat to Denmark and went to a theater in Copenhagen when you were little girls?" asked Hans in deep wonder.

"Of course it is true. You know Grandmother's father was living then and we went to visit him on our vacation. And Grandmother's brother in Copenhagen took us to the Royal Theater."

"I have never been on a steamboat." Hans looked most disgruntled. "And I have been to the theater only once—the time we saw *King Ragnar and Aslaug*. And Anders said that was an awfully dumb play."

"If we go to Oslo for Easter you may go to the theater

—if there is anything playing that is suitable for children."

"Don't worry, there won't be." Hans spoke as a man who had no illusions left. "But, mother, when you write books, you make up what goes in them? Then you lie, don't you?"

"At least the books I write are what we live on," said Mother curtly—but then she had to laugh. "People know that what is in books is not true in the sense that everything has happened just that way."

"Then I think I could learn to write good books, too," said Hans brightly. "Because I can think up an awful lot of stuff, can't I, mother?"

"Time will tell. But get along now—it's already five of five. And you won't go down and wade in the Holme pond, do you hear?"

"But, mother, you said yourself just now that it was not deep enough to drown in anywhere," Hans laughed, then dashed out the door before Mother had a chance to say anything further on the matter.

In April the snow begins to melt in earnest down in the valley. On the slope above the kitchen garden the withered lawn peeped through, a bare spot that grew larger and larger every day. The ski jumps left from the Christmas holidays were only two patches of dirty snow out in the middle of the lawn. Here and there and everywhere as the snow melted Mother found mittens and caps and scarves—picking up a little of everything whenever she went for a walk in the garden to see whether the snowdrops and the daffodils had begun to sprout.

Anders went with her on these walks. He liked flowers and liked their garden, as long as he did not have to be bothered with it. But it was always Anders who brought Mother the first coltsfoot to turn up its bright eye from the edge of some ditch and the first white anemones from the birch groves on the other side of the creek.

The air over the valley was full of the sound of running water. Every creek and every ditch was flooding its banks. It was still freezing cold at night—the creek that flowed through Mother's garden lowered its voice toward dawn, and there was a silvery tinkle in it when the thin crusts of ice forming along the edges broke as fast as they froze. The dogs dashed down to the creek the moment they were let out in the morning and lapped the muddy water, rolled in the wet, dead grass, and raced down to the big birch at the farthest end of the garden to tell off the magpies that lived in it— whereupon the magpie family replied point for point. But up in the mountains there was a fine ski course

still, and the Easter holidays brought a new invasion
of tourists to all the hotels. And every Sunday Anders
disappeared early in the morning—he had to go up to
the mountain and make use of the skiing roads while
there was still something left of them.

About three o'clock one morning all the apple trees
in the orchard were full of red-winged thrush that
whistled and sang. It was light as day, and the sky the
pale gold of dawn. The red-winged thrushes were only
passing through—as soon as there was food to be found
up in the forest they would leave. The chickadees that
had kept themselves around the house all winter, living a life of ease in the Christmas sheaves, now went
off in twos to play and sing their ti-ti-ty, ti-ti-ty and
bustle in and out of all the birdhouses looking for
housekeeping quarters. One day there were hundreds
of chaffinches on the bare spots in the garden. They
would wait here for their wives—the female of the
species always arrived from the south a week later than
the male. Mother and Thea scattered birdseed for
them, and tried to keep the cats indoors. But that was
easier said than done—to keep cats indoors in the
spring.

Chestnut cats are the best mousers but the worst cats
for killing birds, the peasants say, and this held true for
Sissi. But Sissyfos pretended there was nothing in the

world that interested him less than bird hunting. Then
one day he disappeared and did not return. The boys
maintained that he was out courting. Finally there
came a message that the hired man at the Rand farm
had shot Sissyfos. He had caught him in the act of
killing all Mrs. Rand's baby chicks out back of the
barn. Now, it appeared that Sissyfos had been a great
hunter. Only he had been clever enough never to hunt
in his own neighborhood but went on his predatory ex-
peditions in other parts of the community.

"At least he died a death worthy of a tomcat," declared Anders.

But Hans wept a little over Sissyfos. And Mother
felt bad because she feared Tulla would miss her very
own cat.

Every day the roar of the cataract could be heard
more clearly all over the little town. The mist-smoke
lay like a white band along the river's course, but underneath the bridge in Main Street it came down like a
shower upon the passers-by.

One Sunday noon Anders came home from the skiing hill with his cap full of blue anemones and violets.

"There are thousands of them up there, mother. . . .
Yes, we have been hauling snow for skiing until today,
but today is very likely the last time we use the hill this

year." He sighed. Then, "Mother, one month from today is the Seventeenth of May," he announced radiantly.

"But aren't you going to study now?" Mother reminded him as he prepared to go out again as soon as he had finished his dinner.

"Haven't time. I've got to run. There's a committee meeting today."

"Committee meeting?"

"Entertainment committee, of course—that's what I'm on. But I'll try to look over my lessons tonight a little."

A pig is big when it can put a curl in its tail, and a boy is big when he can serve on a committee. Hans and his friends, Ole Henrik and Magne, were also on a committee, they said, though they seemed to represent no one but themselves and their work consisted chiefly of counting their savings—which grew less week by week. But they had great plans on how to improve their finances by the Seventeenth.

"You know you'll get a half crown in Seventeenth of May spending money, Hans," Mother reminded him. "That is enough for you to go to Maehlum on."

"Ole Henrik gets a crown . . . from his grandmother," whispered Hans, a pained look on his face.

"That's nice for Ole Henrik."

"Don't you think Grandmother will come up for the Seventeenth?"

"I haven't heard anything about it."

Hans appeared to be deeply grieved over Grandmother's faithlessness.

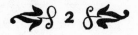

FINALLY ONE NIGHT CAME THE RAIN. FOR THREE SUC
cessive days it streamed down, mild and still.

"Mother," said Hans triumphantly, "I thought it
was just something people said. But now I can hear it
—the grass grow."

Yes, the soft, sweet sound of falling rain that
awakens the smell of earth and the first green blades
of grass that are breaking through the earth. . . .

"Yes, it is true. Now we can hear the grass grow."

The fourth day the sun came out and before evening all the birches were golden with tiny buds shaped
like mouse ears. By next morning these buds had
turned into tiny leaves and the trees stood there—green.
Hans went with Mother when she went out to pick
some of the first young birch leaves and white
anemones for the Sunday dinner table.

"Mother, tell me the story you told me last year. About the pants-coat."

"Dear me, have I told you that one? That was in a reader Aunt Signe had when she was little."

IT WAS A STORY about a father who was explaining to his two little daughters, Kirsten and Else, the meaning of the Seventeenth of May. To illustrate, he reminded Else of the coat she had that was made out of an old pair of his pants. Else did not like this coat at all. It did not fit her, although Mother had done the best she could with material that had been cut originally for an entirely different purpose. All the children in the street shouted "the pants-coat, the pants-coat" whenever she wore it. And the day that Else got a new spring coat which had been made just for her was the happiest day of her life.

The union with Denmark had become a kind of pants-coat for Norway. It was so many hundreds of years ago that the two countries had united that people had almost forgotten how it happened in the first place. Queen Margrethe, mother of Olav Haakonsson, the last descendant of Norway's old royal family, was also the daughter of the King of Denmark. When her father died, Margrethe got the Danes to select her son Olav to be Denmark's king. Olav inherited the crown of

Norway from his father. But Olav died quite young. And so Queen Margrethe got both the Danes and the Norwegians to choose a little German prince, who was the son of her niece, to be king of Norway and also king of Denmark. And after him came other German princes who had nothing more to do with Scandinavia than be descendants of Danish princesses who had married in Germany. And in a measure these foreign kings united Norway and Denmark into one kingdom. But Norway soon became the stepchild in the union. It was a poorer land than Denmark, and so far-flung and difficult to rule—Norwegians were known to be head-strong and obstinate—that public officials and clergymen considered it almost like being banished to be sent to Norway. Finally, when the last king that ruled over the "twin kingdoms" lost a war with Sweden, he was forced to cede Norway to Sweden.

But the Norwegians did not want to be ceded to anyone. They remembered their ancient right. Norway was not a part of Denmark, but an independent kingdom. It was the Danes who had chosen to unite themselves with Norway when they chose Norway's King Olav to be their king also. And they knew every man in Norway had always had greater freedom than people had had in Denmark and Sweden. There the peasants were subjects of powerful proprietors and noblemen, but in Norway the peasants had never been serfs. Even when they were renters and cotters, they had only to pay certain sums to the owner—they did not have to give him their services. He could not command them to become soldiers. The Norwegian army was a people's army, and in the Danish-Norwegian fleet it was the Norwegians who had always made the best sailors and marines. The Norwegians did not want any Swedish pants-coat. They knew it would never fit them.

Representatives from all over Norway gathered at Eidsvold to discuss how they could rescue our independence. While the Swedish army and the European powers, by means of blockade and threats, sought to force Norway to accede, the fathers sat at Eidsvold and worked out a statement that expressed our ideas about the rights and justice, the dignity and honor of the Norwegian people. On May 17, 1814, Norway's constitution was adopted and the men at Eidsvold swore to protect our right to live under laws "sewn" to meet our own requirements. That was our new spring coat. . . .

"And no matter what has happened since in Norway's history, and what may happen in the future, remember, dearly beloved children, the Seventeenth of May is and will remain for us, in the words of our old song, the 'most blessed of all our days.'"

"Do you think Grandmother ever helped Aunt Signe with that lesson about the pants-coat?" Hans asked, with a wise smile.

"I honestly don't know. Norway and Denmark have so many good things to remember from the days of the Union—things of which both countries can be proud. Grandmother preferred to speak of these things."

"Is it true, mother, that when you were little only boys were allowed to march in the Seventeenth of May procession?"

"I can even remember the day when it was called 'the Boys' Seventeenth of May Procession.' You see, in the olden days it was considered improper for girls to appear in a public parade. When I began school most girls even went to girls' schools, and certainly most parents would never allow their daughters to be in a parade. But Grandfather and Grandmother put me in a coeducational school, and that was a year or two after it was recognized that all Norwegian children, girls as well as boys, had a right to take part in the Seventeenth of May procession. So I got to be in it all those years I went to school. The girls all wore garlands of green leaves and spring flowers on their heads instead of hats. . . . It was a shame they dropped that custom. They were a lovely sight."

"Oh, mother, I wish I had a photograph of you with a garland on your head," Hans said reflectively. "You must have looked wonderful."

Mother was so touched and flattered that she completely forgot she had a bone or two to pick with Hans that afternoon. But she was *sure* Hans had not been calculating in his compliment. . . . Poor Hans. It always chagrined him so whenever Mother had to let him know she was displeased over something he had done.

No one understood how Tulla knew it was the Seventeenth of May, but every year, as that day drew near, Tulla seemed to know it and became eager and excited. Perhaps it was the new, stronger sunlight, or that the world had become green again, that reminded her. For she gazed at the treetops and her eyes followed the birds winging their way over the garden. Also from every bush could be heard the singing and trilling of many birds.

"Flags," she said, and "music" and "car." Her face beamed with delight.

The significance of the day she certainly could not know. No one could penetrate her little world with stories of pants-coats and liberty or death. "Fatherland" —she had no idea of the meaning of that word. Still there was probably not a child in Norway who loved his country more than Tulla did. When Mother promised that tomorrow they would go for a long drive up into the mountains, she could not sleep that night for sheer joy. Rivers, waterfalls, trees wringing their tops in the wind—Tulla threw out her arms toward it all and rejoiced. She could not possibly know what the flag meant, but no one could doubt that Tulla loved the Norwegian flag above all else in the world. When it was raised on the pole in front of the house she wanted only to be allowed to sit quiet and behold it, hour upon hour, staring at the tricolored cloth streaming in the wind over her head.

"Red, white, blue," explained Anders to his brother. "Those are freedom's colors. The French and the English and the American and the Dutch flags—these are all red and white and blue."

"Yes, but the Danish flag is only red and white," said Hans. "And the Danes are just as free as the rest of us."

"The Danish flag is the oldest in Europe," said Mother. "It goes back to the time of the Crusades, and it was a Church banner at first. In those days people did not think of freedom as we do now. Freedom then meant deliverance from the power of the devil, and the cross was the symbol of that deliverance. That is why the Danish flag is marked with the cross."

"Grandmother says it fell down from heaven during

a battle the Danes were just about to lose to some
heathens. God threw it down to them, and so they won
the war."

"Yes, that's how the legend goes. It is a beautiful
story. That was why we kept the white cross on the red
field in our flag—and also to commemorate all the Norwegian seamen who had sailed and fought under
Dannebrog. But we drew that blue stripe straight
through the cross because we wanted to live under today's colors of freedom."

It was the custom in that little town for the boys in
the Junior College to begin the celebration of freedom,
or independence, day by staying out most of Seventeenth of May Eve shooting off firecrackers and making
as much racket and commotion in general as they possibly could. That is to say, all the boys in town took part
in the uproar, but according to tradition, it was the boys
from the Junior College who had started the bad habit.
But bad or not, it had now become a privilege and a
right for the youth of the town. So when the new Chief
of Police hit upon the idea this year of banning the
shooting of firecrackers at night, most of the parents
took the boys' part. Wrathful fathers wrote letters to
the local papers, and indignant mothers assured all and

sundry that they most certainly would not sit up all night to see that their sons did not slip out. The Chief of Police was from Kristiansand, and was therefore halfway an alien in this inland town, so what business did he have trying to change the town's customs? Of course it was a nuisance—this racket at night, but when the town's fathers and grandfathers and great-grand-fathers had put up with it, one would think the man from Kristiansand could keep his ideas to himself. . . .

Thea was out visiting some friends and Mother was sitting at her writing table that afternoon, when she noticed a strange odor in the house. It smelled almost as it did when Anders was busy stewing his ski grease, but his skis had been put up in the attic for that year. Better go up and see. . . .

In the kitchen stood Anders supervising Ingeborg and Mari Moen. Anders was pouring a black powder into cone-shaped containers made of newspapers. A heavy cord that looked like a candlewick hung from the tip of each. Ingeborg was wrapping a new layer of news-paper around the cones, making them look like big pears. Mari Moen was dipping the pears into a pot on the electric stove. There was something in the pot that looked like ink or tar. When they discovered Mother in the doorway, Ingeborg looked as if she were suffering from an acute attack of bad conscience, and Anders exuded embarrassment at Mother's tactlessness.

"What in the world are you all doing here?"

No answer. Nor did Mother say any more. She had not participated in the newspaper controversy but at bottom, she also felt the Chief of Police was a troublesome fuss-budget, and agreed with the mothers who maintained that one could not shepherd grown boys day and night.

"Where is Tulla?" Mother asked, distrustfully eying the black pear-shaped objects.

"I thought Tulla could take her nap in her chair out in the garden, it is so nice today," said Mari Moen. "I tucked her in good all around."

Behind Anders's back, she nodded toward the pails of water at her side. "Madam does not need to worry— about Tulla."

Mother realized she ought to withdraw. . . .

"—but of course it is true, as the Chief of Police says —noise and uproar near the hospital or the Home for Tuberculars cannot be tolerated," Mother remarked out of the blue as they sat at the supper table.

"Oh, let up, mother. We never did carry on in those streets. We always used to stay in Main Street, and on the market place and around there."

Anders's eyes were dark with virtuous indignation

"It may be that this year the center of disturbance will be farther south. In the direction of Björnstjerne Björnson Street, for instance."

That was the street in which the Police Chief lived.

"Well," said Mother, "if you get away with it . . . If you don't, you brought it on yourselves, you know."

MOTHER WAS AWAKENED BY A FEARFUL CRASH. BE-
yond the dark treetops the sky was beginning to turn
yellow, and in the birch grove a pair of thrushes chattered their protest against the disturbances. It was not
yet three. . . .

Another. It was probably that old cannon in the
artist's garden down the hill. Apparently he too had
taken the boys' part against the authorities—naturally
enough, for he himself had been a schoolboy in the
town once upon a time. There it went again! Banging
and thundering came from far and near in the spring
night, from firecrackers and other, more powerful
explosives.

Mother peeped into the boys' room. Anders's bed
was empty, but Hans lay sleeping like a rock, oblivious
to the shooting of the cannon.

The next thing that awakened Mother was Anders

96

racing like the wind between the bathroom and the boys' room. He was getting into his Boy Scout uniform. He stopped at the door when he saw Mother was awake.

"Believe me, those bombs we made yesterday—they made a terrific noise, mother."

He sat down in front of Mother's vanity, arranging his green kerchief and combing his hair, though it was already as flat and slick as if the cat had licked it. His cap sat at the proper angle—"on three lice only," as the boys said.

"And you know what, mother? We had been down Church Street, and, can you imagine, Nils, Arve and I ran smack into the arms of a cop—Clarin, it was—and this new constable. I'll tell you we went into high gear then! And do you know what Clarin said to the other one? 'I didn't recognize them,' he said. 'I don't think they live here in town. They're probably some gypsy kids from around Leirvika.' "

Hans peeped in. "May I get up now too?"

"No, you go to bed and sleep a little longer, Hans."

Mother had in mind his white sailor suit. It would not be worth while for him to put it on until just before he started down to school.

"But aren't you going to have breakfast before you go, Anders?"

"Haven't time. We'll stop in at Petra's after the procession, I imagine."

The lake lay bright and pale below the hills, with ripples marking the currents. The ridge on the other shore was mirrored in it. The sun stood high in the heavens—it was nearly seven—as Mother walked down to see the Boy Scout Parade. Through the quiet morning air came the first clear notes of the horns. The official opening of all such celebrations was the band's playing of chorals and national songs from the church steeple for half an hour. Mother hummed the words as she walked:

> *Gud signe vårt dyre fedraland*
> *og lat det some hagen blöma*
> *Lat lysa din fred frå fjell til strand*
> *og vetter fyr varsol röma.*
> *Lat folket som bröder saman bu*
> *som kristne det kann seg söma.*

> God bless our glorious fatherland
> And make it bloom like a flower
> Let Thy peace shine from mount to strand
> Long winter flee spring's shower.
> As brothers let our people dwell
> In Christ find strength and power.*

* Translated by Haakon Rust, Music Division, Library of Congress.

The town's largest silk flag had been raised over the market place. A light fair-weather breeze lifted the heavy flag and waved the Boy Scout banners in greeting. The Girl Scouts were there too in their navy-blue uniforms, and the Boy Scouts in khaki shirts and trench caps. There were not many of them, and not many people had gathered to see the parade. The Seventeenth of May is a long full day and most people saved their strength for later events. But it was a pretty sight. . . .

Anders was the standard-bearer. The flag hung down and covered his face and shoulders. For only an instant did the wind lift it so that Mother caught a glimpse of his face, tense with earnestness. She recognized him by his narrow, straight figure, with the heavy leather belt that supported the flag stick.

Then the parade was over and the boys and girls all went their various ways.

There was not a house in town without a flag today. When Mother reached home Tulla was already standing at the window, dressed in her new peasant dress, and shrieking with joy every time their flag rolled out upon the breeze.

Soon afterward the first little Seventeenth of May procession came marching past the garden fence. It was made up of the pupils from Kringsjå School on their way down to the meeting place. The children waved their little flags high toward the green leaves on the overhanging branches and sang in their high, shrill voices:

"*Jeg vil verge mitt land, jeg vil bygge mitt land—*"

"I will defend my country, I will build my country—"

They had no band, for Kringsjå was only a little country school, but they shouted and hurrahed, their voices shrill and glad.

Hans buzzed through the house like a bee in a bottle.

"My cap! Who's seen my cap? And my wallet? Where's my Seventeenth of May ribbon—and my flag?"

Then he sniffled and wiped his nose on the sleeve of his white sailor suit.

"Hans! Handkerchief, Hans!" shouted Mother and Thea and Ingeborg, each from her door, and each waving a white handkerchief at him as he scurried down the garden path.

When they came indoors again, Anders stood in the dining room, dressed in his third outfit for the day. Now he had on his blue sailor suit.

"Mother," he began, "do you know where my flag is—and have you a Seventeenth of May ribbon for me? . . . Oh, Thea, I couldn't find my garters, and there

---

are no clean handkerchiefs in my drawer "

"The way you boys can *never* look after your own things. It's always Mamma this, and Mamma that, or someone else this, and someone else that, who's supposed to keep things in order for you?"

"That's what womenfolks are for, isn't it?" muttered Anders, but then he smiled apologetically. "Thea, you couldn't fry me an egg or two, could you? It was so crowded at Petra's I couldn't get my hands on anything but one solitary cupcake."

Finally they were rid of Anders too. Mother would have time for a little breakfast and a cup of coffee before Böe arrived with the car. Mikkelsen and Mrs. Mikkelsen, the neighbors, had apparently already gone down, for Leddy, their beagle, was howling disconsolately and pulling at her chain. Njord and Neri sat happily thwacking their tails on the floor—they knew their folks would never chain them up and leave them. One could positively see them smile. Suddenly they leaped up, barking. They had heard Böe's car down the road.

He had decorated the car with festoons of little paper flags and placed bouquets of blue and white anemones and red tulips in the vases inside the car. Tulla was helped in, where she sat bouncing with excitement. Njord and Neri stood on their hind legs in the car and looked out, each from his own window, although Njord ducked down and curled up at Mother's feet as soon as he heard and smelled the first "grasshopper," or jumping firecracker. Njord could not endure the smell of gunpowder. Neri growled ferociously at every boy who was shooting off firecrackers.

The town had five thousand inhabitants—or four thousand nine hundred forty-six, to be exact. And every single one of them must have been out to see the children's procession, and at least as many had come in from the countryside round about. Already a wall of people stood along the route the procession was to take.

There are probably not many little children in Norway who have not prayed to God in their evening prayers on May sixteenth that He must let there be sunshine tomorrow. And no matter what the weather was—for it sometimes rained or even snowed—they must, and *would* wear their new spring outfits on the Seventeenth. They howled and shrieked if their mothers fussed at them "to put on your raincoats," "wear your winter coats." . . . But on such a Seventeenth of May as this one, with the lake free of ice and lying blue below the hills, with the blue sky and sunshine over the newly sprung leaves—then it was pleasant to see everyone in their new light summer clothes. It was pleasant to see them as they stood waiting for the children's procession, holding in their arms their youngest children, who were too small to be in the procession, so they could wave their tiny little flags as brother or sister went by.

Most of the girls were dressed in the glensman's costume of the Gudbrandsdal region. Their everyday dress is so pretty and practical—a skirt of narrow-striped red and black and gray wool, a Scottish plaid bodice, full white sleeves and a headdress of starched white batiste knotted becomingly. Some wore copies of the old styles in the museum and these were glorious—large-checked or broad-striped skirts embroidered all over with flowers, vests of yellow or red or green silk brocade, and on their bosoms or at their throats large filigree brooches. And everyone—men, women, and children—wore a bow of blue and white and red silk ribbon on his breast.

Böe found the parking place he knew Mother liked for viewing the procession—in Main Street at the corner near the school. From there one had a view down the hill by Horsters Institute, where all the old men and old women peered out the windows from behind the flowering potted plants. As the procession approached, it looked like a blood-red fluttering river—except that the river was running uphill—before it swung beneath the big old hardwood trees in Main Street.

Bom-bom-bom bom-bom, bom-bom-bom bom bom bom bom came the drums in the distance. It was "Sonner av Norge, det eldgamle rige" ("Sons of Norway, That Ancient Kingdom")—the old national anthem known as the "crowned anthem." It was highly pretentious, and it was hardly ever sung any more, since Björnstjerne Björnson wrote his songs that said so smoothly and simply how Norwegians feel about the country that is theirs. But in this little town it was a tradition that the band leading the Seventeenth of May procession play "Sonner av Norge," and never anything else. And the children who usually knew no more of the old song than the first line, sang disrespectfully—

"Ompa-di-pompa di ompa-pompa-pompa,
Ompa-di-pompa di trivio-livo-lei . . ."

The brass horns shone and the drumsticks beat donk, donk, donk. Behind the band came the town councilmen in morning coats and high hats. The Chief of Police strutted, erect and solemn, and half the town whispered and buzzed as he went by.

"Wonder if he's angry now?"

And Mother thought, a little conscience-stricken, that it was probably wrong, really, to let the children do as they like nearly always. Of course we also did as we liked, but if we got caught we were punished, so we

---

learned the price of having our own way. Our children might get the idea that such things could be done at no cost. . . .

Up the hill came the flood of red flags, carried high by children's hands. The junior college came first, the old familiar school banner waving over the stream, the teachers in their university caps marching alongside. Directly behind the banner, came the seniors—the graduating class of boys and girls who would enter the university this year. They wore red caps, red ribbons across their chests, and carried little canes with red bows. They hooted and shouted at the top of their lungs. The seniors considered the Seventeenth of May their own special day. They had finished their written examinations, though they would not know the results until the end of June. And the more reason they had to fear the day of judgment the more hilariously they celebrated the Seventeenth of May. It had happened that now and then a boy or girl had celebrated the Seventeenth of May as a senior twice, and even three times in succession.

Thea and Böe stood up in the car and waved.

"Did Madam see Anders? Tulla, did you see Anders?"

Mother had caught but a glimpse of the boy. He and all his classmates had donned monocles—presumably an idea of the Entertainment Committee.

Tulla was equally happy whether she saw her brothers or not. She shouted about the flags and the sun and the music, and now she recognized the melody of "Ja, Vi Elsker Dette Landet" ("Yes, We Love with Fond Devotion"). And she squeezed Mother's hand in joy.

Now the public, or elementary, school was coming, headed by its own band. And they *could* play, these white-clad boys! Some of them were so little they could scarcely be seen for the horn or trombone they played. Everyone waved at them and shouted "hurray!" for the boys' band in the public school was the pride of the whole town. It was unbelievable, considering the size of the town, the number of children that passed in review behind the public-school banner. The littlest girls were sweet beyond words, with their skirts and starched white kerchiefs that made them look like tiny peasant women.

It was a long procession, for the near-by country schools—Skogen, Kringsjå, and Åsmarka—were in it too. When the procession was over these children from the country would have all forenoon to walk around town and look at the fine things in the windows and everywhere else, so they were of all the children the happiest today.

As soon as the last school had passed, Böe started looking for a place to park where Tulla could see the whole procession once more. He did not even ask Mother's permission—both Böe and Thea considered the day Tulla's. And when she had seen the procession for the second time, Böe drove to the market place.

There, beneath the town's huge silk flag, the speakers' stand had been erected, and as the school children streamed in and gathered around beneath the golden maples, the mass looking like a bed of red-white-blue fuchsias in the sunshine. Around them stood a wall of people—fathers, with hats in hand and a baby on one arm, mothers, both hands busy with little children. All began to sing when the children started up the song.

> *Ja, vi elsker dette landet,*
> *som det stiger frem,*
> *furet, veirbitt over vandet*
> *med de tusen hjem.*
> *Elsker, elsker det, or tenker*
> *på vår far og mor*
> *og den saga-natt som senker*
> *drömme på vår jord—*

Yes, we love with fond devotion
Norway's mountain domes

Rising storm-lashed o'er the ocean
With their thousand homes.
Love our country while we're bending
Thoughts to fathers grand
And to saga-night that's sending
Dreams upon our land . . .*

The speaker was a young instructor. It was not easy to hear what he said over here where Böe's car stood, for they were not allowed to drive nearer than to the corner of Church Street. But toward the end of the speech a gust of wind carried a few sentences clearly and distinctly to where Mother sat.

". . . and as you leave here, children, you have the entire day ahead of you for having fun, and for thinking up mischief. That is as it should be, in my opinion If you can learn that back of all the fun that is truly fun, and back of all real and carefree joy, there lies always a deep and deadly seriousness. It is only those things in life which we have bought dearly that become so precious to us and the source of all our joys, our light hearts, and our hearty laughter. People complain nowadays that our youths are irresponsible and frivolous today—you have all heard that. I do not know, but I

* *Songs of America and Homeland*, ed. by Chas. W. Johnson, published by Silver Burdett & Co., New York, Boston (1906).

would be happy if you could come into possession of the true lightness of heart that men and women achieve when they have had to try their strength and come to know themselves—know they can take the hard way, and can bear the heaviest burdens . . ."

Then it was over, and the market place became a single mass of children, elbowing their way amid the grownups, threatening to put out people's eyes with their flagsticks. Some were hunting their relatives, some going home with friends to have hot chocolate, but most of them were bound for the town's four pastry shops. For that was part of it—that after the procession the children were to be allowed to eat innumerable cookies and tarts and quench their thirst from all the hurrahing and all the dust they had swallowed.

Streamers, or "air serpents," of colored paper sailed over people's heads and firecrackers spluttered and crackled underfoot. Hans now bobbed up at the car, perspiration rolling from his face, his white sailor suit not exactly white any longer—and three handkerchiefs lost.

"Do you want to come along and pick violets, Hans?"

It had become a fixed custom that after the procession Tulla was to have a long drive beside the lake.

Hans crawled in—and they had scarcely got out of town before the boy sank down there in the front seat where he sat with Böe and went to sleep.

It was strange and quiet along the country road to-day. Almost no cars, no carriages, no one out walking. The road along the lake was already white with dust, as in summer, and there was somehow a Sabbath still-ness over the light-green landscape, even though there were people working in the fields in many places. Two heavy bay horses were before a plow and overturning the rich, dark soil on a hillside facing the sun. There was the soft creaking and jingling of harness as they turned at the end of a furrow, the man behind the plow clucking and shouting to them. Cows and sheep grazed in the pastures under the birch trees and juni-pers, and at one place a flock of frolicsome goats sprang about on a rocky hill below a large farmhouse. There was an odor of newly sprouted birch leaves and of dung that lay in heaps in the fields waiting to be spread out. Flocks of dirty-gray crows and decorative magpies in black frock coats and white shirt fronts ransacked for choice tidbits.

And at every farm they passed, Tulla threw out her arms and shouted "flag, flag." For there was not a home, large or small, that did not have a flag raised at full mast today. Far on the other side of the lake, one could see them like tiny red flames against the light hills and the dark evergreen forest up along the ridge.

THE SEVENTEENTH OF MAY

Every other minute Mother or Thea shouted to Böe to stop. One or the other of them had seen something—a slope densely dappled with the greenish-yellow clusters of Virgin Mary cowslips, a brook that wound and ambled through a little opening in the forest, its banks abloom with the first bright yellow marsh marigolds. On a ditchbank Thea found bumblebee flowers, and in a dark crevice in the cliff, where dirty snow still lay beneath the spruce firs, Mother came upon the last blue anemones.

Every time the car stopped the dogs leaped out. They had to drink from every brook, roll in all the grass—and finally Njord smelled sheep in the forest, and set out after them like one possessed. His forebears for several thousand years back had been shepherd dogs, and it was in his blood—when he saw sheep he had to go after them and drive them into a bunch. But sheep owners somehow did not appreciate having strange dogs take on that function and Mother was always on pins and needles for fear some unpleasantness with the owners would result when Njord hit on the idea of playing shepherd. Neri, the poor little fool, gave voice and set out after Njord—always certain that whatever the big dog did he also ought to do.

At long last Thea and Böe and Mother had the dogs back. For punishment, Mother put them on a leash.

And now, said Böe, it was high time to start driving back to town, if they wanted to see the senior parade.

Hans had slept like a rock all the time—not even the commotion with the dogs awoke him. And he did not wake up until Böe stopped the car on the hill by the junior college.

Along the street people stood waiting, whispering and chuckling expectantly. There were rumors that more than half of the *Senior Standard* had been confiscated by the censor, for one of the stories was so disgraceful that the author was to be banned from the oral examination that was coming up.

"Author*ess*," corrected a prim, elderly lady. "Yes, isn't it terrible? Think of it, they say it is the daughter of Archdeacon Bang in Norddal who wrote it, and it was something simply terrible. Indecent, it was! Her poor parents—they are completely upset. . . . The girl will certainly be suspended and they can hardly afford to keep her in school another year. . . ."

So it was something of a sensation when a group of senior girls in white dresses and red caps rushed out through the school gates and began to sell the much-discussed *Senior Standard*. Ingebjörg Bang, the archdeacon's daughter, was in the lead, and it was supposed to be certain that she would be suspended. . . . Her dress was altogether too short, in the opinion of the elderly lady, and wasn't she bold to wear red stockings and white shoes!

Now the sinner was smiling and curtsying to the Chief of Police and, sure enough, he bought a paper from Ingebjörg! People watched his face as he opened it, adjusted his pince-nez, and began to read.

Mother could not help but feel that the *Senior Standard* this year was rather innocent—the jokes were mild, and the "editorial" as well. But on the last page she found a "detective story" by "Black Peter" which she recognized as something Anders had written last winter for the school paper: a story about someone having broken into Petra's pastry shop and about an unjustly suspected schoolboy who had escaped from the Police Chief's office—with the aid of the Police Chief's daughter, who was in Anders's class.

Mother had got no inordinately high opinion of Anders's writing ability but the story was rather rough on the police. And here it was cooked up and brought up to date as an adventure supposed to have taken place on the eve of the Seventeenth of May. Officially, it was the seniors themselves who wrote the paper, but actually they accepted contributions from both younger school children and—some said—from grownups in town who took advantage of the fact that the seniors, to a certain degree, enjoyed unlimited freedom of speech.

The Police Chief read the "detective story" about himself, and smiled condescendingly. And when Anders and a group of his classmates came out—their features distorted with the effort of holding a monocle in place on their round boys' faces—and began to stroll up and down in front of the row of spectators, he smiled again, all graciousness, even though the boys were mimicking him and his constables to the life. They pulled their faces into the sourest expressions they could muster, and pompously jabbed the large-girthed gentlemen lining the street. . . .

"Don't crowd now—there, make a little room here, here comes the procession—stay back of the line, there!"

And now a great commotion started at the gates. With much howling and yowling, as a crowd of boys carrying "banners" on long poles that were only pieces of cardboard with sketches and inscriptions in colored crayon—the boys' own comments on the affairs of the community and the world. More or less witty they were—mostly less. But there was a firm conviction among the townspeople—as in every other town where there was a junior college—that "our seniors" were the wittiest or—as some would say—the most impertinent in the entire country.

The first "banner" depicted the "Monarch of the Mountain," an ancient eccentric who lived in a hut on the mountain and who had been appointed game warden for the Eastern Hunt Club. Whether this appointment had been meant as a joke, or seriously, no one had ever been able to find out. But the Monarch of the Mountain on the banner wore a cap and insignia that greatly resembled those of the town's police. As caption the boys had used an old saying: "He to whom God gives a mission, He also gives understanding."

The Police Chief continued to smile—if a bit wryly —and enthusiastically clapped his begloved hands. And since Anders bobbed up just then beside the car, Mother remarked rather angrily that she thought the Chief of Police had taken it all very nicely—"impertinent and disagreeable as you have been toward him. He certainly had a *right* to forbid shooting firecrackers last night. It is not done anywhere else."

Anders lost his monocle in sheer astonishment at Mother's criticism. He looked reproachfully at her and disappeared.

"And now we d better see about getting home," decided Thea. For Tulla did not care about the senior parade—there was no band, only shouting and yelling, and the banners held no interest for her—and Thea was very much interested in being at home when Anders and Hans stopped in to get the cups and spoons they needed, for after the parade all the pupils in the entire school would march up to a meadow beside the falls and have an eggnog party. But it rarely happened that the boys brought home from this picnic the eating utensils they had been allowed to "borrow," and Thea muttered that the trick Anders had played on his mother two years ago, when he took one of the old silver spoons that no one had ever seen since, should not be repeated. Hans agreed and looked indescribably sanctimonious. This was the first year he was old enough to be allowed to go to the falls.

Leddy, poor thing, was still howling on her chain. But now Njord and Neri were so exhausted from all the excitement that they made no objection whatever when Mother chained them too. For from now on the boys would be flying in and out all day long and forgetting to close the gate behind them. And it would not be wise to let the dogs run downtown alone on a day like today.

Tulla's chocolate was brought to her and she was placed out in the garden in her beach chair near the flagpole. But in an instant her eyes closed and she slept

Thea brought the Christmas ham down from the attic and cut some slices from it for the first time and for dessert they had the first rhubarb from the garden. It was the same every Seventeenth of May, for on that day it was impossible to eat at the regular hours. Youngsters, Ingeborg, the boys, people who happened to be in town for the day—they all came and went today whenever they happened to think about food. It was but the matter of a moment to sauté some potatoes and scramble some eggs. The children were satiated with cookies and lemonade and ginger ale and eggnog and maintained they could not bear the thought of food—until they had taken the first bite of the salty and succulent red ham, and then they ate like wolves.

Mother sat with Tulla in the garden in the afternoon. From downtown came the sound of music—it was the citizens' parade starting at five o'clock. But Tulla looked so tired that Mother did not dare take her down again.

The Entertainment Committee—Hans and Magne and Ole Henrik—suddenly appeared coming full speed up the hill. It seemed they had concentrated their activity on the purchase of fireworks—a pinwheel, three rockets, and several boxes of Bengalese matches Now they were busy getting ready for the big celebration tonight, setting up the four giant rockets that were

to be the principal attraction. They tried them first outside the windows of the large parlor, then pulled them
up and tried them farther down the hill—only to move
them several times again. They got an incredible
amount of fun out of this, playing so nicely and quietly
that Mother thought that if only Tulla would let go
her hand she would go get some milk and cookies for
the boys, they were so good. . . .

Just then Anders and a friend hopped over the hedge
down by the road and came storming up the hill. They
too began setting up rockets and other giant firecrackers. Committee Hans & Co. burst out in terrific howling. . . .

"Hush up, little ones. We're not going to hurt your
things. All you have to do is move them down a little
farther."

"Why, you! We were here first. . . . Mother, *shall*
Anders be allowed to move our rockets? We were the
ones who thought of having fireworks here tonight—
and now Anders is going to have fireworks too, just because I told him we had bought—oh, *you!* You're just
aping us, an ape, an ape, that's what you are!"

"Boys, boys! There is room for all of you on the hill!
Hans, it is *fun* that Anders and Johan have rockets too.
Now you will have a great display tonight."

"Yes, but Anders and Johan have many more rockets

than we have—and so it will be mostly *their* fireworks."

"But it was your *idea*. If you had not thought of it first, Anders would certainly never have thought of it."

"Oh, yes, mother, Johan and I decided a long time ago—"

Mother interrupted him. "Now you are to keep still and not tease your brother. If you like, Anders may go in and ask Thea to find some ginger ale and cookies for you."

But for once the boys declared they could not drink any more ginger ale.

"My stomach clunks like a barrel of water now when I run," explained Magne.

It does not become properly dark this time of the year until about midnight, and by then the children had to be in bed. But finally the dusk became deep enough so that the flagpole looked dark against the blue-green air.

The boys were as close as pearls on a string now. Not only had Anders and Johan given their word of honor not to light any of the rockets belonging to the little boys, but they had promised Hans and Magne and Ole each one of theirs. The five of them stood gathered around their rockets, awaiting their public. Ole Henrik's father and mother and Magne's sister and Johan's cousin had been invited to come and see.

Thea had bathed Tulla and made her ready for the night, but she was allowed to come down with her fur coat over her pajamas.

"Look, Tulla—look!"

The first streak of fire shot to heaven, where with a faint explosion it burst into a shower of blue and yellow light drops that drifted slowly to earth. . . .

Tulla was so impressed she neither laughed nor shouted but only pressed close to Mother, almost as if she were afraid. She had never seen fireworks before. And Njord crept under Mother's skirts and lay trembling, but Neri flew around in circles between the boys' legs and scolded with all his might.

It was a splendid display—the entire audience was unanimous about that. And finally, when Hans's pinwheel began to rotate, a spluttering wheel of golden rain over the darkening hillside, Tulla had become so courageous she shrieked with delight. But Njord fled into Mother's lap, big and heavy as he was, and rolled up and tried to convince her he was only a poor little lap dog that should be allowed to hide its head in her hands.

From downtown came the sound of music in the night. There were parties everywhere, and organizations were still parading and playing the national songs. But now at last it was possible to get the boys to go up to bed.

As Mother came into the boys' room to say good night to them the fireworks on Maihaugen, or May Hill, began. Far away over the dark treetops there was a drizzle of red and yellow rain and stardust. . . .

"So now it is midnight, boys."

The boys had to come to the window to look. But soon that too was over. The children's longest and happiest day in all the year was ended. And suddenly big tall Anders put his arms around his mother's neck and kissed her. Then Hans came and wanted to kiss his mother, too.

"Thank you for today. Oh, we have had so much fun! Haven't you had fun, mother?"

PART III

SUMMER VACATION

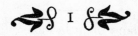

"MOTHER, WHEN SHALL WE MOVE TO THE SAETER?"

"Right after St. John's, Hans."

"Mother," then asked Anders, "Godfather wrote he
and Uncle George are coming to meet me at Ringbu
as soon as the Boy Scout jamboree is over. We're planning a three weeks' camping trip. Could I join you at
the saeter afterwards?"

"Of course. How nice of Godfather and the professor to want you along on their camping trip again
this year, Anders."

"Yes, very nice. But then, of course, you know I
make myself useful too. I am a kind of orderly for them
you see."

Norway is a large, far-reaching country, but people
can live and build homes on but a small part of it.
Along the coast, with its thousand isles and projecting

rocks, lies a garland of little towns, fishing hamlets, outports, and little farms where women and children cultivate what poor arable land there is, while the men and boys are at sea or out fishing. But Norway's interior is one single, enormous mass of mountains. From the backbone ridge, the divide between Norway and Sweden from north to south, run mighty ribs of mountain range with many peaks and pinnacles of which the highest are everlastingly capped with ice and snow. But between lie wide upland moors, gray with lichen —the "Iceland moss"—and green with dwarf birch, and dotted everywhere with the bright glance of water—little lakes, pools and tarns, and little brooks that unite to form rivers that seek their way to the valleys.

As early as September 'come rain and storms that tear the red and yellow leaves from the dwarf birch and snow falls—to lie until midsummer. Snowstorm follows snowstorm the whole winter through, and when day is but a quick blink and the greater part of the twenty-four hours pitch-dark, then the mountains are such that few persons can bear to live there. Still every settlement in Norway has stories to tell from olden days about someone who had been outlawed by the community and fled into the wilderness and built himself a stone hut deep within a crevasse between mountain walls. There he lived for years by hunting and fish-

---

ing. . . . Then there are stories about strange and erratic characters—recluses who, in the olden days, lived on the saeters the year round. The mountains teemed with reindeer and ptarmigan and blue fox and bear and wolverine and provided the fearless hunter with all the food he needed, and all he desired of excitement and adventure.

Not much wild life remains in our mountains and where the outlawed ones once had their secluded refuges now lies one large tourist hotel after another and buses transport the guests up and down the mountain. But still anyone who wants to get away from other people can find room and view enough in the great wilds and moors that still exist.

And nearly every farm in Norway has its saeter in the mountains—a cottage where one or two or three milkmaids live in the summer, a stable for cows and goats, a hayloft where the farmer can store the good, fragrant hay from the meadow until such time as he can haul it down to the valley when there is sledding. In Norway we have never managed to grow enough grain for our daily bread and people have to rely on dairying for the other necessities. And as far back as we know anything about dairying in our country, the farmers and peasants have utilized the mountain pastures by moving their stock to the saeter and feeding them there from the time the grass in the mountain first begins to grow—it grows so fast during the long, light days that you can see the difference in it between morning and night—and until the autumn storms and snows come when summer ends. In olden days the saeter girls had to make cheese and churn butter. Now they have only to milk and care for the cows, for the milk is usually sent down to the creamery in the valley by a milk truck that also calls for and delivers mail every day. In many ways it is easier now to be a saeter girl than in the old days when there was not "a living thing but the animals to see" from one Saturday to the next. On Saturdays there were usually visitors from down in the valley—and the girls were very eager. "Wonder who's coming tonight?" For, true enough, they usually had a friend they hoped would come. . . .

But, though in the last score years or so the saeter ways have become ever so modern, the cows are unchanged. A cow thinks and acts about as her mother and her grandmother acted, generation after generation, for a thousand years. From the first spring day that she is let out of the barn and allowed to graze in the field at home she longs for the mountain. There, she recalls, she is free to graze the livelong day in milewide pastures of short, sweet, and juicy grass, drink from cold, clear streams, rest during the hot midday hours someplace where a breeze cools and helps to keep away the tormenting mosquito swarm. Deep somewhere behind her square brow lurks perhaps a shadow of that fear her mother before her knew—the fear of bear in the mountain. But the cow does not know what it is she fears, for there are not many cows nowadays who have ever as much as smelled the scent of a bear. There is only this unease left—a nervousness that makes a Norwegian cow intelligent and capricious—so that the peasant women say a cow is almost like a person, she is so canny.

Then comes *buferdsdagen,* that day the stock is started up the road to the saeter. They travel day and night. It is impossible to get them to stop along the way. The saeters of many farms lie so deep and high in the mountains that it takes a day and a half or two days to get there. The start usually is made late in the afternoon in order to travel as much as possible by night when it is cool and dew has settled the dust on the road.

After St. John's, and for the fortnight following, herds of stock from farms south of town passed by Mother's garden fences every blessed night. And when Mother heard the faint clang of cowbells in the summer night and the cartwheels creaking in the gravel of the road, she could not restrain herself—she had to throw a dressing gown over her nightdress and run down. Often Hans woke up, but Anders was so busy, now that school was over and the Boy Scout jamboree in Ringbu and the hiking trip with Godfather were coming up, that he slept like a rock. But for Hans vacation was vacation and he slept more lightly, so when he heard Mother get up he tumbled out of bed and trotted along behind.

"Oh, you should at least have put something on," Mother said. "What if you catch cold?"

Hans pretended not to hear—and it was true Mother said such things only because mothers are supposed to talk like that.

Housetops and treetops outlined themselves darkly against the white lake, and the heavens were bluish-white above the dark ridges. It was as light as day out, as if the colors had only fallen asleep; tall irises that were reddish purple when the sun shone on them looked wholly blue in this strange northern light. Hans's sandals turned dark and his pajamas got wet far up his legs as he and Mother walked across the lawn.

"Oh, child, you'll freeze."

Hans climbed up on the panel gate and hung over.

"It's Mrs. Rindal, mother. It's the cows from the parsonage. Mrs. Rindal, Mrs. Rindal," he shouted.

Mrs. Rindal waved and called good morning, but to stop was something saeter people had no time to do.

"Come on, come o-on, come o-o-o-on . . ." came the milkmaid's call. She walked at the head of the procession.

First came the bell cow, followed by a row of reddish-brown brindled and white-spotted cows. The bull and the calves came last. The herd of blue and brown and gray-black goats tripped and pranced, some in front and some behind and some alongside the file of cows, their little bells pinging fine and clear. Finally came two carts loaded with the cream separator and dishes and vats and bedding—and a washtubful of potted plants and a loom too, Mrs. Rindal had on her saeter load. Atop it all sat a big chestnut tomcat beside the driver, looking as if he was the master there. He was a son of Sissi. Mrs. Rindal had got him two years ago.

"Mother," Hans shouted in jubilation, "did you see Mr. Rosenquist. Hasn't he grown big?"

Mother had put her arm around Hans to keep him from tumbling on his head in sheer delight.

"When are *we* starting for the saeter, mother?" he asked, his voice plaintive with longing.

"As soon as the St. Swithin's celebration is over," Mother replied and sighed.

For everyone in Norway longs for the mountains in

summer, exactly like the cows. True, some long more
for the sea. But nearly everyone is so recently sprung
from the peasant, or the fisherman, or the seaman that
when summer comes, with its long days and short,
never-dark nights, they feel in themselves a great longing to search out the place whence their ancestors came
so short a while ago.

"You'd better change into a pair of dry pajama
pants," said Mother, when they got back in the bedroom. "I'll go find some for you."

But when Mother came back with the pants, Hans
was already sound asleep. So she only spread an extra
woolen blanket over his legs. Naturally, Mother did
not really believe either that anyone could catch cold
from standing outside watching the stock pass by,
saeter bound.

THE BOYS' REPORT CARDS COULD HAVE BEEN WORSE. They *could* have been much better too, of course. But both of them passed, and that was almost more than Mother had dared hope for.

The little town where Hans and Anders had their home lies directly on one of the main routes of summer vacation travel. And all who passed through the little town had to stop off and see Maihaugen, the big outdoor museum for which it is renowned.

The story of Maihaugen is a story in itself. Anders Sandvig was the name of a young Norwegian dentist who had won a reputation as a scientist in his field. He had just accepted a creditable appointment abroad in Europe when it was discovered he had tuberculosis, and the doctors said that if he wanted to live he had to go back home to Norway and settle down up there someplace where the altitude was high and the air dry and clean. Sandvig felt this was like being sentenced to a living death. Should he give up his work in a university abroad for a dental practice in a little country town—where he had to keep office hours one day a week or so in hotels and at farmhouses along the valley, for farmers certainly could not make a trip to town every time they had toothache. . . . Little did Sandvig suspect at the time that Fate had assigned him a life's task that would make him one of Norway's most deserving sons.

At that time—fifty years ago—a new era was reaching into the quiet Norwegian valleys, where the life of the people for a thousand years had progressed so smoothly and so slowly that the peasants themselves fully believed they lived as their forefathers before them had always lived. For even though each new generation added its experiences and discoveries and improvements to the value of their heritage, the peasants always claimed that the poor little improvements *they* had contributed, or had seen come, were nothing in comparison with what their forefathers, in their wisdom, had contributed. Then came the railroad, the telephone, better roadways, the water power in the cataracts was harnessed, new ideas and new people streamed in on the old social order. The peasants became bewildered, uncertain of the worth of the values they held and had depended upon before. Soon they began to imitate the new. That was good in many ways. They learned much that was sound and true. But they lost their confidence in their own inheritance. Blindly, and with uncritical eyes, they abolished the "old-fashioned." Much was not worth preserving, of course, but much, much more was good and tried— the fruits of a people's experiences through a thousand years in how to best manage life in a harsh and difficult land.

The old dwelling houses on the farms were built of logs and thatched with turf—snug and warm in winter, and airy and cool in summer when the heat of the imprisoned sun between the mountainsides turned the air in the valleys suffocatingly hot. Now the peasants began letting these old houses fall into ruin or tearing them down to build houses of clapboard instead, with verandas and tiled roofs—flimsy, ugly, cold in winter, and all too warm in summer. They bought cheap furniture of town style and moved their fine old things into the attic or sold them to antique dealers from town or from outside. They began wearing clothing from the stores and discarded their homespun things—the strong, practical working clothes and the gloriously colorful garments they had for festive occasions. Worst of all, they gave up their old food and their plain cooking. Instead of hard, coarse bread and a rich abundance of milk and butter and cheese, and meat and fish from their own brine barrels, they began drinking coffee many times a day and eating soft white bread and margarine, and bought canned goods when things were to be particularly fine. It was not strange there was work enough for a dentist in the valley.

Anders Sandvig realized that something was wrong. He looked at the old farmhouses rotting away. How skillful the carpenter's work had been, how beautiful they were in every way, how cheerful it must have looked inside, where a few heavy pieces of furniture, carved and painted in gold and many colors, shone against the unpainted log-brown walls. He bought such an old house and moved it down to town, rebuilding it in his garden. He bought others. It became a passion with him to collect, bring home, and salvage all he could of the old glory that had been in the valley. He bought everything he could lay his hands on that was old—clothing, furniture, old tools, the peasant's plows, the housewife's milk pails and her loom, the cobbler's awl and boot tree, the carpenter's ax, weapons from the early days—the archer's bow, swords, and old flint-lock muskets, hunter's rifles, and soldier's gear. Soon he had no more room for it all in his own home. So he bought Maihaugen, a wooded knoll beyond the edge of town, moved his collection there, and the com-

munity museum for Gudbrandsdal had been created.
It grew year by year. The town took it over, and
Sandvig became the director, living for it, expanding
it, and enriching it as a picture of the valley's life in
the old days. He rebuilt the large farm called Björnstad
—a farm larger and grander than many a nobleman's
estate elsewhere in Europe, with its four dwelling
houses, its barns and stables for all kinds of farm animals, its storehouses, threshing rooms, and granaries.
There were almost thirty buildings altogether. He rebuilt also a poor little farm from the very summit of
the ridge, from the mountain's edge, that gave evidence
that skill in handicraft, good taste, and a feeling for
everything that was fine and beautiful was shared by
rich and poor alike in those days. He reconstructed
houses that displayed the development of Norwegian
home architecture from the Middle Ages to the Motor
Age; he reconstructed an old church and a chapel from
Catholic times; he set up and equipped the old crafts-
men's workshops, the hunting lodges, fishing huts,
gristmills and querns. At Maihaugen the Norwegian
people could learn what they should cherish of their
inheritance at the same time that they advanced and
learned and discovered new things—learning why and
how it was that they were at one and the same time the
most conservative people in Europe and the most au

daciously progressive. Maihaugen became a model for other outdoor community museums in Norway, with Sandvig gradually training a school of young men and women scientists to carry on his work.

But it costs money to run and develop such a museum. The townspeople did what they could to support Maihaugen and one of the most effective means they had devised was the event that took place at St. Swithin's.

St. Swithin's is in actuality the period that lies between the end of haying and the beginning of harvest —a few weeks when the peasants have their only breathing spell of the summer season. But Sandvig had moved St. Swithin's up a few weeks, to the beginning of the summer vacation period, when the stream of tourists would be passing through by train, or car, or afoot, on their way to the mountains or the seashore.

This year both Anders and Hans were allowed to "assist" at the St. Swithin's festival. Mother brought Anders Dr. Sandvig's suggestion that he take part in the dancing of the quadrille in a uniform of 1814. One of the numbers of the program this year was to be an exhibition of old dances. But Anders smiled regretfully and shook his head—and Mother, who knew he was a mediocre dancer and a worse actor, was in full agreement with him. He could certainly "assist" much more effectively by serving as an orderly along with the other Scouts.

But Hans had enthusiastically accepted a role in the play that was to be given, and Anders observed dryly that since that youngster never did anything but clown, he should be a great success when he really had a part to play. Instantly Hans assailed his brother.

"Oh, *you!* Mother, why may Anders always be so disagreeable toward me? . . . *You!* You say that just because you stood around like a stick-in-the-mud and looked dumb that time you were in a play."

So they tussled a bit, and then they made up again, and Anders gave Hans that old bowie knife with the brass mountings as a contribution to his brother's costume. It would certainly look fine on his rear!

It was not precisely a leading role in which Hans had been cast, nor was it a particularly difficult one. He was to be one of the children of Gudbrand of Lia, and Mother was to be his mother in the play as well. But Mother had succeeded in borrowing a gorgeous child's costume for him from the museum—a jacket and pants of white homespun, all the seams bound with green and embroidered with black and a red-checked vest with brass buttons. Headgear was unnecessary, for the children of Gudbrand of Lia certainly never had unnecessary clothing. And naturally they went barefoot. . . .

At this point Grandmother protested. She had come on a visit and had brought with her Little Signe, who was also to have been one of Mother's children.

"If you *will* let that boy run barefoot all through Main Street and all around Maihaugen where people drink beer and throw the bottles in the bushes and perhaps break dishes and glasses so that there is broken glass all around he could cut himself on and perhaps get blood poisoning and *die*—then I can't stop you from risking your son's health and perhaps his life, for you are his mother. But *I* am responsible for Little Signe— her mother has entrusted her to me—and she may *not* be in your foolish play."

"Oh, Grandmother . . ." Hans was almost in tears. "Poor Signe! Oh, let her. Why can't she ever have any fun, just because you have to worry so much about everything?"

But Little Signe remarked patronizingly that she would much rather not have to trudge through town— when she could ride in the car with Grandmother and Thea and Tulla and see the parade, and afterward go to Maihaugen with Grandmother and have hot chocolate.

The theme of the exhibition this year was "The Norwegian Folk Tale." A professor from Oslo had come up and would lecture on our folk tales, in the street procession that opened St. Swithin's would pass all the familiar figures of the folk tales, and the comedy that would be staged was a dramatization of the folk tale about Gudbrand of Lia.

"But, mother . . ." Hans cried, completely aghast, as Mother came down dressed in her costume, "you look like a . . . a— Your face is dirty! And your apron is torn right in front on your stomach, and the way your hair looks— Mother, you can't go through town like *that*!"

"You silly goose," laughed Anders. "Don't you know Gudbrand of Lia's old woman was a dirty slattern?"

But Hans could not quite reconcile himself to the idea of his mother looking so frightful.

"Dear me, mother, you look as if you were on relief," he groaned.

"Don't you see, in real life they *were* on relief," said Anders. "The rest of it was only make-believe."

Grandmother said nothing, but she eyed her daughter disapprovingly as she set out with her flock of barefooted children.

THERE WAS ONCE a man named Gudbrand, and because he lived high up on the mountainside they called him Gudbrand of Lia, or Gudbrand of the Lea. They were very poor but Gudbrand and his wife were so happy and contented with each other that no one had ever heard them exchange an unfriendly word.

One day Gudbrand had to raise some money, and there was nothing for him to do but to take their only cow and go to town and try to sell her.

"Oh, well," said his wife, "I am really glad of it. Then I won't have to get up at daybreak every day to care for her and milk her, and go chasing all over the hills looking for her in the evening. Yes, it's a good thing to be rid of this cow."

That night as Gudbrand was coming home with his neighbor, telling him what he had done that day, his neighbor slapped his leg and said:

"Well, if your wife never bawled you out in all the years you're married—when she hears this tale she'll get so raving mad that it wouldn't surprise me if she socked you right in the eye."

Gudbrand said, oh, no, his wife never got angry with him. This the neighbor could not believe, and so they made a wager. The neighbor was to go in with him and hide on the porch and listen to what the woman of Lia said to her husband. And if she was satisfied with the way he had done things this time too, he would pay Gudbrand one hundred crowns, cash in hand.

It was pitch-dark before Gudbrand got home, and

his wife was almost beside herself with joy when he stepped into the room.

"Oh, God be praised that you have come! I was just about to be afraid something had happened to you. Come now, and have something to eat— Thank God, I have you home once more. It is so bleak and dreary here when you are away. . . . Well, how much did you get for the cow?"

"Well, as it turned out I didn't sell the cow for *money*, for while I was walking around the market place I saw a man standing there with a little glossy yellow mare—and I got such a desire to own this mare that I traded the cow for her."

"You don't say! Well, well, so we have a horse here at Lia! Well, it is about time. Now we don't have to go begging our neighbors to lend their horse every time we are to plow, and we won't have to carry the hay on our backs. And we can ride to church on Sundays, like other fine folk. Run, children, and put up your father's mare."

"But you see, mother, I don't have the mare with me after all. For when I had walked a little farther at the market and looked around, I saw a man with such a pretty pig for sale. And so I traded the mare for that pig."

"Well, well, well, so we have a pig! Well, that's

what I always wanted—a pig to feed the scraps to. Then we'll slaughter it at Christmas and have us a barrel of salt meat, so we'll have a piece of rind in the house all year. Oh, you Gudbrand, you Gudbrand, the likes of you as a man to think of and care for his wife and children is not to be found. Run, children, and put in our pig, then—"

"No, wait a minute! You see, I don't have the pig either now, because I traded it away for a sheep, a real, fine, plump sheep."

"A sheep, you say? Oh, you are so clever and thoughtful I think the likes of you is not to be found in seven parishes. What would we do with a pig, anyway? People would only say that over here at Lia we eat up everything we have. I can shear the sheep twice a year and have her just the same, and I can get lambs from her to slaughter and salt down. Hurry, children, go out and get my sheep."

"Hm. I don't have this sheep either now, for I met a man who offered to trade me such a fine goat he was leading—"

"Well, you were exactly right there, Gudbrand. A goat is much more useful. Now I will have milk for the children just as if we had the cow, and socks of goat hair are what we need up here more than wool socks.

Children, go get the goat."

"Oh, but— There was a man who had such a fine goose he wanted to sell . . . and I wanted so to taste roast goose for once in my life. It's wonderful, I've heard."

"Yes, why shouldn't we treat ourselves to a little roast goose for once? You did exactly right when you traded yourself this goose. We'll have goose grease afterwards and I'll have the feathers and the down for my little head pillow. Children, run out and bring in our goose, then."

"Hold on a bit, there, and I'll tell you something. I traded the goose for a rooster—such a fine rooster he was, and I thought it would be nice to have a rooster on the farm."

"Yes, that's true. A rooster crows every blessed morning, so it is as if you had bought an eight-day clock. We certainly will be just as happy even if we never taste roast goose, and I can fill my pillow with sedge grass. So go out and bring in the rooster, children."

"The only thing is, I don't have the rooster with me, either, mother. There was a man at the market selling such fine apples. And I thought it would be fun to bring some apples home for the children, so he gave me a peck of them for the rooster."

"Oh, oh, oh, did you hear that, children? No children in the world have a kinder father than you. What would we do with a rooster, anyway? We are our own masters and can stay in bed as long as we like in the morning and the rest of the time we can go by the sun. We will have to see to getting these apples in, so the children can taste one tonight."

"Hm, that's a little bothersome, you see, but since I'd been walking all day in town without a bite to eat, either wet or dry, I was so hungry that at last I went into Kaffistova and traded me a meal for the apples."

"Oh, thank God, you did that! Just think if you should have had to walk all the long way home without having had anything to eat. No, that would have been all too terrible. Thank God, you are home again, safe and sound, you kind, good husband of mine. As long as I have you, I can get along without a cow and horse and pig and sheep and goat and goose and rooster and apples—oh, oh, I am so glad I can't tell you."

"So there. What do you say?" cried Gudbrand of Lia, opening the door to the porch and beckoning his neighbor to step in.

Well, the neighbor could do nothing but say that Gudbrand had won the hundred crowns and he laid them on the table. And so they got what they needed this time, anyway—Gudbrand of Lia and his wife.

It had rained early that day, and the three barefoot children had to wade in all the puddles they came to and feel the mud bubble up between their toes. When they arrived at the place where they were going to meet, they looked as if they had lived at Lia all their days.

The meeting place was the general merchandise store at the north end of Main Street. When the pageant started the sun was shining. The musicians led the way with their violins and clarinets playing the fine old bridal march of Dalsbön. First came the king—the professor who was going to give the lecture. To achieve the proper kingly figure he had stuffed himself with pillows and eiderdowns both front and back. With the gilded crown on his head and the long-stemmed pipe in his mouth, he looked truly majestic. Next came the princess, riding a large, dappled-gray horse which Askelad, or Cinderlad, was leading, for of course he was always the one who won the princess and half the kingdom in all the folk tales. She was lovely with a silver-gilt crown on her flowing yellow hair and dressed in the red bridal costume from the museum, resplendent with silk and glimmering gold lace. The pastor, the parish clerk, the sheriff, Gudbjor Langlar, the wisewoman with her following of gypsies, rich Per the Pedlar and the Devil, arm in arm—they were all there. Storekeeper Lie was well cast as Gudbrand. He was tall and thin and wore a long green coat and a black hat with a brim that flapped down over his face. He led the horse and Mother, as Gudbrand's wife, followed with the cow.

They had assured Mother that the cow was an elderly animal, not in the least nervous, and gentle of disposition. But when the cow came out on the street and saw the solid wall of spectators along the sidewalk she stopped, eyed the crowd distrustfully right and left, and looked as if she did not want to be in the procession. Mother tugged and pulled at the rope, and the *huldra*, or pixy, who followed behind—the long cow's tail dragging from underneath her green skirt and with a young pig in her arms—gave her a slap on the rump. . . . Well, thought the cow, she could try, so she started.

After the *huldra* and the pig, came the boys and girls with the sheep and the goat and the rooster. At the beginning there had also been a goose, which the young girl in the crinoline costume from Lysgard had offered to carry. But the goose had hissed and fought and struggled so to get loose, flying right in the faces of some of the spectators, that it had created a lively little panic before it got away and disappeared into a side street.

People stood as tightly packed as on the Seventeenth

148

of May, but now they were not only townspeople. There were many strangers in sports clothes—foreigners from the hotels, school classes of children with their teachers from the schools outside town, Oslo people whom Mother knew. They made bad enough worse by shouting words of encouragement to her every time the cow became a problem. For the whole thing had become too much for the old cow. One moment she balked, the next moment she started determinedly up the sidewalk among the people—and at every mood the children screamed most realistically. The musicians played the bridal march, the sheep bleated, and the pig squealed. . . . It became quite an undertaking to walk through all of Main Street and up the hill to Maihaugen. On a corner Mother caught a glimpse of Anders. She got an unhappy impression that the boy was furious because his mother was appearing thus like a clown in the streets of their town. But Anders assured her afterwards that if he had looked glum it was only to keep from laughing, for if he had ever started laughing he would surely have gone into hysterics.

The stage was a raft on the largest tarn on Maihaugen. It was beautiful beyond words: the evening sun gilded the spruce forest and the old brown houses, and on the bright water, where the wooded ridge and the houses stood upside down, sailed large white swans, breaking the mirrored picture. The crowd stood close packed along the lake's edge, and the singing and the music rang out fine and clear in the still air.

The professor stepped forward. He looked rather odd, for the pillows and the eiderdowns had slipped out of place, so he was no longer exactly a kingly figure. But he stood straight, his crown on his head, gesticulating with the long-stemmed pipe which he held in his hand. And his lecture was excellent.

The journey through town had turned the children utterly wild. Now they discovered that when they jumped and ran the whole raft moved and water splashed in on the stage floor. So they jumped and ran all the more. Mother had a frightful time trying to keep a little order, and never succeeding in getting very much. But the public thought it was part of the play and loudly applauded everything the children hit upon. The play went very well.

Only once—while Gudbrand told of the apples that had also disappeared on the way, Mother happened to look at Arnljot, Hans's friend whom she had borrowed to be one of her children. He stood with a strange, hard, and bitter expression on his handsome face. His real mother was not unlike the wife of Gudbrand of Lia—good and pretty, but a little careless in looking after what was her own. Last year, when Arnljot was seven

years old, he had to start school and the teacher asked
him about his father.

"My father is in America," said Arnljot. "He went
over twelve years ago, and since then Mother hasn't
heard from him."

Poor Arnljot, he did not understand why the other
boys in his class began to laugh. But during recess they
took pains that he found out. It occurred to Mother
that Arnljot knew that this story about Gudbrand of
Lia had another version that was not so nice—a version
that the children know better than many frivolous
grownups.

Mother determined that Arnljot and the little girl
she had borrowed in place of Little Signe were to come
with all the other players over to Hjeltarstuen, where
Dr. Sandvig had invited all his assistants for supper.
The sun had gone down now, and the tar barrels and
torches around the tarn had been lighted. Lights also
shone from all the old houses where there was fire in
the fireplaces and all the candles were aglow. The
sound of organ music and psalm singing from the
lighted chapel floated out into the summer night.

Mother and her flock needed in high degree to tidy
up a bit so she wandered around looking for the dressing room that was to have been devised for the players'
use. Soon Little Signe and her friend, Anne-Marie,

turned up—fine as a flute in their new peasant cos-
tumes, with white starched kerchiefs, red stockings,
and silver-buckled shoes. When Hans and Arnljot
realized that the girls intended to go along with them to
the party at Hjeltarstuen, they protested indignantly.

"You haven't done a single thing for Maihaugen—
just had a good time while we worked!"

But Anne-Marie only scoffed. The professor was
her godfather, and he had said they must be sure to
come.

The two little girls had been to the restaurant with
Grandmother and had had as much chocolate and as
many cakes as they could eat. Yes, they had seen the
procession, and Grandmother had screamed out loud
when she felt certain the cow was about to gore Mother
and every child to death. But Thea thought Mother
had not done so badly with the cow. One had to remember that Madam was unused to animals, and it was
a troll of a cow they had given her. Only Tulla had
not enjoyed herself very much. She could not understand why there were no flags in the parade today.

It is said Hjeltarstuen was built by a man who had
been in Copenhagen as royal guardsman at the time
Norway and Denmark were united under one king.
And there was a distinguished lady—some said she was

one of the king's natural daughters, others that she was a Danish countess—who had fallen in love with the handsome soldier, and he with her. When Ola Hjeltar came home again to his estate, she ran away and came with him, and in order that his distinguished wife should live in keeping with her position, he built Hjeltarstuen. The parish registers say that Ola Hjeltar was married to a clergyman's daughter, but people in the valley prefer to believe the story about the princess of Hjeltar. At least the house is one of the grandest at Maihaugen. It had not been built for everyday use; it stood on the farm and was used only for weddings and other such festivities. They could afford such things at Hjeltar. It is built of the choicest logs and the woodwork and carving and painting that went into it are among the best examples of old Norwegian folk culture.

To enter it this evening was to enter the home of the king in all the folk tales. In a corner of the room there burned a fire of pine roots that cast flaming-rose light over the shiny, smooth-worn floor and over the walls hung with tapestries in the fashion of the old days. The long refectory table, made of one single plank over six feet wide and twenty feet long and brilliant with candles in silver and wrought-iron holders, groaned under the weight of pewter dishes heaped with food, silver tankards full of ale, dram glasses and rare old bottles and decanters. Over in the fireplace hung a large kettle of chocolate for the children and old copper pots of coffee for the grownups. The king and the princess walked about welcoming the guests. The king looked rather depleted now, for he had taken out all his stuffing; and the princess had laid aside her silver-gilt crown. It was so heavy that it had made a fiery red mark on her forehead and given her a splitting head-ache.

But when the newspaper photographers came, she had to put it on again. All the children pushed forward to sit in the middle of the front row. They wanted to be sure their pictures would be in the paper early next morning, although Hans protested: "Little Signe and Anne-Marie have absolutely no right to be in the picture." At that moment the photographers set off their flash bulbs—and it was very evident from the pictures in the paper that the ragged youngsters of Gudbrand of Lia and the elegant little girls of Hjeltarstuen were not at all good friends.

"*There* is something to paste into your scrapbook, Hans!" said Mother, when she saw them.

The youngsters made up when they were invited to

the table, and the maids brought in large plates of pip-
ing-hot cream waffles. They ate as if they had been
starved for a week—Little Signe and Anne-Marie as
well.

From outside came the sound of dance music.
Young people played on the lawns and the gypsy girls
came in to tell fortunes and sing and dance their gypsy
dances. But the children were not interested in the
gypsy girls for now the professor had seated himself in
front of the fireplace and had lifted Anne-Marie and
Little Signe up on his lap, one on each knee. The children gathered in a circle around him. He was going
to tell them stories. The grownups moved over—for the
professor was the man who could tell the old folk tales
in such a way it seemed they had never been told before.

But everything has an end, except the sausage,
which has two. And even an evening such as this one
had to end sometime. The candles had burned down
in their holders, and in the fireplace there remained
only a heap of coals. Dr. Sandvig himself gave orders
that they could not lay on more wood and the volunteer
fireguards who were going to keep watch in all the
houses tonight came in and sat down with the guests.

That meant people could go now.

"Oh, tell one more story, Uncle Professor. Just a tiny one."

"It will have to be a short one, all right," declared the professor.

THERE WAS ONCE a fox who lay on a sunny hillside and slept. A hare came hopping along, shouting and singing, "I am so happy, so happy," and stumbled right over the head of the fox.

"What is the matter with you?" said the fox. "Why are you making so much noise?"

"I am so happy, so happy," said the hare, "for I have been married."

"That was very nice for you," said the fox.

"Oh, no, not so nice," said the hare. "For my old woman was a troll, and she was old. She had many rings on her horns."

"That was too bad," said the fox.

"Not so bad," said the hare, "for she had a little house."

"That was nice for you," said the fox.

"Oh, no, not so nice," said the hare, "for the house burned down."

"That was too bad," said the fox.

"Oh, no, not so bad," said the hare, "for the old woman burned up too."

Outside it was as dark as summer nights ever are in Norway. Housetops and treetops stood etched against the clear blue-green sky and from down by the tarn glowed the last red embers of the tar barrels and the torches. The fireguards slipped like shadows everywhere, and down by the entrance it was impossible to find Böe's automobile among all the cars that stood there. But Böe found Mother with her drove of youngsters without difficulty and got them packed into his car, all of them.

Anders was sleeping when Mother and Hans came into the boys' room. He slept so soundly he did not even stir when Mother stumbled and nearly fell on her nose over his clothes scattered all over the floor. And Hans was so tired Mother had to undress that big boy and wash his face and hands just as if he was a little baby. But then he put his arms around her neck and kissed her good night, exactly as he used to do when he was little.

"—so *now* we can go to the mountains soon, mother."

"Yes, I think we can go sometime next week."

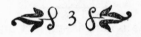

THE ODOR OF NEW-MOWN HAY DRIFTED IN FROM ALL
the meadows of the valley the afternoon that Mother
and Hans drove up. Mowing machines clattered on
every farm, and hayrakes jangled softly across the
fields. The river flowed broad and full, flooding the
fields in the bottoms—on the little isles out in the water
only the tops of the alder trees and the roofs of barns
and sheds showed—and the water was bluish-green
now, for the thaw had started up on the snow fields of
Jotunheimen. Wild ducks, each with its train of
ducklings looking like puffs of down on the water,
swam in the stream.

It was true midsummer now. The light-green tips of
the spruce-fir branches were already long and from the
woods came the smell of that little twinflower, the linnaea. From where the road lay through mountain
passes, it could be seen flowering on the steep cliff

walls, and on every ledge grew spreading tufts of the white and yellow saxifrage, and in the cracks and crevices, bluebells nodded in a wealth of ferns.

"Oh, mother, isn't it wonderful for people like us who are going to the mountains?"

Mother thought of Tulla. It was always sad to leave her—but it was impossible for Mother to find the peace and quiet for work at home in the summertime. There were always so many visitors. But, Mother thought, Thea was there, and Thea cared for Tulla as if she were a lump of gold. Grandmother was there too, and Grandmother always thought of herself as in charge of Tulla and of Mother's house. Actually, it was Thea who was in charge of Grandmother, pampering her with all her favorite dishes and serving her tea and coffee in the garden many times a day.

They had been driving along the river for an hour or so when Böe swung off the main road and the car began to climb toward the heights. This saeter road was narrow and steep, and they had not yet reached the top of the mountain when the water in the radiator began to boil and Böe had to stop beside a brook and refill the radiator with cold water.

Mother and Hans got out. Deep below them the valley widened out like a bowl, with Losna Lake at the bottom. Baklia, dark with evergreens, here and there a little patch of meadow and field around a little farm-house, was already in deep shadow, but the tableland, above the hillside, was flooded with afternoon sun that lighted up the little gray saeters with a light so strong the cattle that far away in the mountains were bright red and white dots and little lakes shone blue and bright. Far to the north one could glimpse gray mountains, their summits crowned with white snow fields.

"Look, Hans. Do you think it is as beautiful anywhere in the world as in Norway?"

But Hans had no time to gaze at the scenery.

"Boy, oh, boy, what strawberries, mother! Oh, Böe, can't you wait a little while? I see some so *big* . . ."

Hans was scrambling over the rocks along the brook. Böe smiled. He could certainly wait a little while, he said, but they must remember they had the greater part of the way still ahead of them, and the people at the saeter would probably like to have their guests arrive before too late in the evening.

"Here, mother. They're all for you. Aren't they good? Have you ever tasted such delicious strawberries?"

The woods were turning sparse. Wind-fallen trees with roots in mid-air reminded one that winter storms take harsh toll up here. The spruce firs were either thin and stunted and bearded with moss, or they were pudgy little bushes that huddled together in little vales

and sheltered places in the land. Moss and lichen cov
ered the rocky ground, broken here and there by brown
tufts of heather and huckleberry bushes. Then the
woods ended and before them lay the plain, the road
looping around bright lakes and winding around bluffs
and crags where the slopes were gray with rockfalls and
the flat plateaulike tops white with reindeer moss.

The sound of wind and rushing streams that ran between growths of stunted gray and green willow filled
the air. Between the crags in shielded valleys stood
mountain birch with gnarled white trunks and fragrant
bright foliage. Little birds flitted in and out of the
bushes, and on rocks along the road sat the stonechat,
cackling and jabbering. In sun-warmed crannies in the
cliffs grew the monkshood, or helmetflower, with its
steel-gray leaves and blue-gray blossoms. And where-
ever a flat of sweet, juicy grass appeared in all the waste-
land, or wherever green slopes tumbled down toward
one of the small lakes, or followed a creek, saeters lay
in groups. From all directions out on the tableland
came the dull clang of cowbells and the light tinkle of
goatbells.

Some of the saeters were old, with long, low, turf-
thatched log cabins that hugged the ground, defying
storms and lashing rains. Some were new, with houses
clad in clapboard and painted red, and roofs of cor

rugated iron or tile. Occasionally there was a cottage, shining new with fresh log walls, and with verandas outside and flowers planted on the sod roof, and an automobile in a shelter behind the cottage—summer homes of people from town and from Oslo. But there were not many of these in this mountain area.

Girls outside the saeters and women and children at the cottages waved to them as they drove by. Hans waved back.

"We're going clear to Krekke saeter, we are," he called.

They drove and drove. Down a slope where the woods took hold again, up and along a tearing river of bog-brown water, and then out once more upon the plain. Finally, after a swing through steep cliffs and crags, Böe pointed and said:

"These are the Goppoll saeters, unless I'm mistaken."

There seemed to be twelve or fourteen of them lying in a row below the crest of the mountain ridge that blocked off the Goppoll saeter area to the south. This ridge did not appear to be very high, for the incline was gradual. But if one tried to walk it one would realize how high it is. Below, the plain spread out like a shallow bowl again. It must have been seven miles wide and ten miles long. To the north cliffs mounted slowly upward, and saeters lay on those steeps wherever there was grazing, but these were the saeters of another community. The divide between them was the river, Big Tromsa, that nosed its way down toward the valley through swamps and a wilderness of stunted willow and dwarf birch. But to the northeast, high, naked, gray mountains blocked the view—the boundary between the saeter mountains of the Gudbrandsdal folk and those of the Österdal folk.

The sun lay almost on the ridge to the northwest and shadows fell far across the lea. The little brown saeter cabins shone like copper in the evening glow and the grass in the fields was brilliantly green. Around every saeter house there is always a little enclosed field, for the peasants must use the dung from the saeter barns for something, and in these patches they grow their finest hay, hauling it down in winter by sled, together with the moss and other feed they have collected in the course of the summer. For the use of persons who come up to the saeter to do the winter work, there is a special house, called the *lunnbu*, which is built particularly solid. It was this winter cabin at Krekke saeter that Mother had rented for the summer.

As they drove up they met the cows coming home to the barn, the bell cow in the lead, followed by the file of cows and the calves and heifers that walked nicely too, learning to do everything the way the grown cows did. Last came the bull. The milkmaids stood outside the gate, calling.

"Come on, come o-on, come o-o-on . . ."

Krekke saeter, they said when Böe asked, was—yes, Krekke saeter was the last saeter before they came to the Björge saeter.

"It's a new house painted red, and there's a new winter cabin above the field, so new the walls are still white, and the roof is just plain dirt. You can't miss it."

A slim, long-legged little girl with braids down her back came and threw open the gate. Then she ran away across the greensward, where three other little girls stood in a row beside the cabin wall. And in the doorway of the saeter house stood a thin little woman with deep wrinkles in her forehead, kind, pale-blue eyes, and light hair. It was hard to say if her hair should be called blond or gray, or how old she might be.

"Well, come in, and welcome," she said. "There'll be something to eat right away. It'll be pretty plain compared with what you're used to, Sigrid, but Sigurd, he said I should do the best I could, so I'll have to try."

Her name was Hanna. She was the dairy woman at Krekke saeter.

"That will be a lot of work for you, Hanna," said Mother, "to have both the cows and us to look after.

But we'll try to be as little bother to you as we can."

The roof of the winter cabin rested almost on the lintel of the door and under the eaves hung a whole row of swallows' nests. Enormous, clamoring, yellow rimmed mouths filled the little opening of each nest, and swallow parents flew in and out with some last servings of midges and flies for their greedy children.

"Oh, mother, lift me up so I can see the baby swallows."

"Not now. We must not frighten our swallows. And you know people say the parent birds do not want a baby bird that human hands have touched; they throw it out of the nest."

"Mother, I shan't touch. Can't I even *see?*"

"Later, perhaps, when the swallows have become used to our living here."

There was a commodious hall and two rooms in the cabin. The furniture was of the simplest, but in the front room a rocking chair had been added and a table that Mother could use as a desk. And there was a wide bed with lovely homespun woolen blankets in black and red check. But until Anders came up, Mother observed, it would be best if she and Hans both slept in the inner room. There were two beds there with the same pretty checked woolen blankets and pillow slips and sheets with wide crocheted insertions.

"Mother, isn't it pretty here? Don't you think it'll be iovely to live here?"

Hanna had started a fire in the cookstove that stood in the bedroom. When Mother had unpacked the essential things from their suitcases, she borrowed two empty margarine pails from Hanna and went down to the spring for water. The four little girls still stood in a row along the saeter house wall, and a short distance beyond stood Hans, his hands thrust to the very bottom of his pants pockets. The children eyed one another silently and with great reserve. They were the daughters of Sigurd Hole, the farmer whose saeter it was, explained Hanna, and their names were Johanne and Janna and Jöda and Little Mari. They came forward, one by one, gave Mother a hand and curtsied nicely, but still without uttering a sound.

"My name is Hans," announced the boy, and then they came forward and shook hands with him too. Then the five children went on with their wordless game.

"Well, *værsogod*, please, come in and have something to eat," invited Hanna.

"Oh, how good it smells here, mother!"

Yes, it was the real old-fashioned saeter smell of milk and whey and butter and cheese.

"Why, I do believe you make your own cheese here at this saeter!"

"Yes, so we do."

The saeter owners at Goppoll had not yet reached an agreement with the creamery down in the valley on delivery rates and such things, Hanna explained, and the roads had to be much better before one could begin bringing the milk down. But it would probably be the last year they made cheese here.

"It's less work for the girls, but I don't know," said Hanna. "You see, they come for the milk before five in the morning, so if the cows have got it into their heads to stay out until late at night, and you have to milk and strain and cool the milk, it means fussing around all night. Yes, you can sleep all day then, but it's not the same. Besides, it isn't very nice to have to write and ask them to send back with the truck every last drop of cream a body might need for the coffee, or for a little baking a body might decide to do, and then to have to ask for butter and cheese and everything! We old-timers, we've always been used to living a little well the time we're up at the saeter. No, I must say I like the old way better."

This was evident from what was spread out before them. Hanna had laid places for her summer guests at one end of the long, unpainted dining table under the windows. There was fresh-baked bread and fine *flat-brod*, a large butter dish of newly churned butter molded in an old carved wooden form so that it looked like a piece of sculpture with roses and lilies in bas-relief. There was goat cheese and the white cheese made from the goat's milk curds and two kinds of dried, homemade sausage, and coffee and milk and cream in enormous pots and jugs.

It was a pleasant saeter house, with copper and stoneware on open shelves along the walls; in one corner a kettle for cheese making that certainly held its fifty quarts of milk and in the other a bed with embroidered sheets and homespun blankets. Hanna even had flowers in the window—a row of green-painted cans with rose balsamine growing in them. The floor was strewn with freshly chopped juniper, and branches of dwarf birch were stuck everywhere along the shelves, around the mirror, and over the fireplace.

Hans ate and ate, while Mother and Hanna talked. The four little girls had sat down on the seat under the south window. Johanne did nothing, for she was supposed to be a sort of second milkmaid here, explained Hanna. She was a big girl, nearly twelve years old, so she had a right to take it easy when they were through with the evening chores in the barn. But Janna was

knitting a sky-blue sweater. She was nine, so it was almost like being on a vacation for her to be here, but her
mother had supplied her with yarn and said she should
knit some school sweaters for herself and Jöda this
summer. Jöda was six, and she too sat struggling with
a little piece of knitting—a scarf, it was going to be, if
it turned out to be anything, Hanna explained and
laughed. Little Mari only scratched the mosquito
bites on her arms and legs and peeped at the strangers.
She was no more than four.

The clear summer evening's dusk lay over the little
lea as Mother and Hans went out to stand awhile by
the gate before the boy had to go to bed. It seemed like
daylight out, for the sky was blue-white still and water
blinked in every direction out on the plain. But bushes
and hillsides and irregularities in the land flowed together in strange darkness, and below the mountain
ridge on the other side of Big Tromsa, a row of light-
points pierced the dusk.

"They're late with their work at the Amot saeters,"
said Hanna, who had come up and stood beside them.

"Oh, Mother, smell how good it smells."

The saeter smell—the smell of wet bog earth where
the cows had tracked through the grass, the smell of
wood smoke from the saeter chimneys, the good warm
smell of cow and the rank odor of goat, the bitter-sweet

fragrance of young birch and willow, wet with dew, and the fine and fleeting smell of shy little flowers hidden in the grass.

"Mother, what is it that's making that noise?"

"It's the golden plover," replied Hanna. "Back of that little hill you see, there straight to the south, there's a little lake, and a pair of plovers have built their nests there."

Something white—a large grayish bird—suddenly came rushing directly toward them—then swung aside, and up, circled over the housetops, and then came at them again, as if it wanted to strike them.

"The snow owl," said Mother.

"Yes. There are such a lot of them this year. They hatch out there in the rocks below Hogtind. They have probably hatched the second brood already. They strike at everything light. It's my kerchief it sees. They say it'll be a lemming year when the snow owl hatches two broods. And it's true we've seen more lemmings around this year."

"Oh, Mother, do you remember the last time it was a lemming year? It was the year I was five years old, and Ulla and Ingvald were with us, because Aunt Ragnhild was ill. You remember, Ulla and I were so terribly sick with the lemming sickness that we had to throw up in your lap before we felt better. Mother, if this is a lemming year, we'll probably be sick in the fall?"

"The last time we had a lemming year we had **not yet** piped water into the house from the waterworks, so we had a well. This year it should not be so bad."

In lemming years, when those small rodents multiply beyond all bounds, they eat the grass down to the very roots, and everything else that is edible up in the mountains. Then they move down to the valleys. They move in hordes and travel straight ahead, stopping at nothing, and going around nothing they may encounter on their way. Automobiles run them down by the hundreds, and dogs and cats kill them right and left, but the horde forges ahead and never swerves. When they come to a body of water they swim and masses of them drown. The dead bodies putrefy and contaminate all the brooks and rivers and wells. Mother remembered the last lemming year very well. She herself was ill for six weeks while she cared for three children who had jaundice and diarrhea and fever and vomited all day long. Thea boiled all the water, but it did not help much. Only Tulla remained well. Thea could, of course, keep her from drinking any water at all. She got only pop and ginger ale for two months, and Tulla had nothing against that.

"Hans, it is almost midnight. Come, let's go to bed."

The water in the margarine pails was pleasantly

warm. Mother helped Hans undress and had him stand in a little galvanized tub while she washed him all over his body.

"Oh, mother, do this every night. Undress me and bathe me. And when I've gone to bed you can sit beside me and tell me stories until I fall asleep."

"Why, Hans, you who always want to be such a big boy? And you are too, by the way. Eight, next month."

"Phewy. That's only when I'm home. I don't want Thea and Anders to make fun of me. But when there's only you and me I don't have to be so big."

He staggered into the pajama pants that Mother held out for him, and tumbled sleepily and sweetly into his mother's arms.

"Now put me to bed and tuck me in the way you used to when I was little."

HANS CAME STORMING IN TO MOTHER WAVING JANNA'S
sky-blue knitting.

"Oh, mother, pick up these stitches that have been
dropped. I pulled out one of Janna's needles . . . and,
mother, may we borrow some thumbtacks?"

"Thumbtacks? Are you mad?" asked Mother, cast-
ing her eye over the damage to Janna's sweater. "I have
no thumbtacks up here."

"Oh, yes, mother, just look and see. Maybe you have
some among your writing things?"

And sure enough, miraculous as it seemed, in a tin
box where Mother kept such things as tape and rubber
bands, she found a package of thumbtacks.

"Oh, mother, you just ought to see the playhouse
Janna and I are making. Come and see."

Mother sensed that she would not have any peace for

173

working this morning. She might just as well go and see what the children were doing.

They were out by the woodpile and the playhouse was, to put it plainly, the little old house from behind the barn. Sigurd Hole had built a new one, more comfortable and roomy, while he was building on his saeter the year before. The old one stood amid piles of kitchen stovewood and chunks for the fire under the cheese kettle. Pine roots and gnarled trunks of white-barked dwarf birch lay waiting to be chopped into firewood and this fate also certainly awaited the old outhouse. The door had already disappeared. But now Janna and Hans were elevating it to the rank of a fine house. Boards were laid on the seat with the unambiguous holes in it, and Janna had spread some paper napkins over them. She had a whole cigar box full of napkins which she had saved from Christmas-tree parties at school and activities at the mission house. She had a thick pack of pretty Christmas cards too and these were to be put up on the wall by means of thumbtacks. Hans ran bringing in "dishes" he had found—parts of a lovely blue glass sugar bowl and fragments of flowered cups and plates.

"I have washed them in the creek, mother. We found them on the rubbish heap, but they are absolutely clean now."

The youngsters had rolled two chunks of tree stump into the "room" and there was no space left for anything else.

"*Værsogod*, mother. Do sit down. There, isn't that ni-i-ce? You shall be invited to our party when Hanna is through with the cheese. She has promised to give us some whey and cookies and coffee and sugar lumps. And Little Mari and Jöda are kind of like our children, you see."

Johanne had more than enough to do. It was she who washed the floors and dusted up at the winter house and down in the saeter house. And afterward she stood and stirred the cheese in the big cheese kettle with a large wooden ladle that was longer than herself, her narrow back swaying from the hips and her shoulders circling and circling. She worked steadily, like an experienced dairymaid.

Goat's-milk cheese is actually not cheese at all—or so the experts say. For when the milk has been warmed so that the rennet can be added, and the milk begins to separate, the casein, or the stuff from which cheese is made, is fished out of the kettle and set aside. This mass, which people here in the valley call *kjuke*, is made into several different kinds of white cheese, but it also tastes good eaten fresh with rich milk and sugar and cinnamon on it for dessert. The whey left in the cheese kettle is allowed to stand and cook by the hour until it thickens and turns a reddish brown. All the time someone has to stir it, scraping the bottom of the kettle. It pays to be especially careful toward the end, when the cream is added, so that the mixture does not burn. By afternoon there is nothing left in the big kettle that was brimful of milk that morning but a clump of reddish-brown dough in the bottom. It is chiefly lactose, or milk sugar, and it is called *myse* or *myssu*.

Hanna would lift this dough up into a wooden bowl and when it had cooled sufficiently, she would work it with a large paddle, and knead it with her hands until the dough was smooth and pliant. She would stand outside the saeter door to do this work—when it did not rain—and the children swarmed around the bowl, filching bits of the sweet, lukewarm dough. They did not get much, perhaps, but always more than their stomachs could handle. Finally Hanna would press the mass into wooden molds. Three or four pounds of goat's-milk cheese would be what she got out of two milkings—the morning and the evening—less what she had set aside to get cream for butter and other household use. By that time nine hours of hard work had gone into the cheese, not to mention all the wood that had been burned under the kettle.

Not so many decades ago, this entire tableland that held the Goppoll saeters, and thousands of other such saeter mountains in Norway, were clad with great, dense spruce forests. Everywhere stumps remain, rotted and overgrown now with white moss and blueberry bushes, and in all the clumps sheltered by knolls and hillocks, and along the creek beds, little shoots of spruce appear and now and then a little fir. But the winter storms on the naked mountain dwarf them and keep them down. Many of these are old trees already, but they have had to resign themselves to growing only in girth and to looking like bushes with thick trunks and close-set branches. And over all the plain, down in the heather, grow flowers which really belong in the forest shade. Exposed to the strong sun up here, the flowers have deeper colors than those in the valleys. The linnaea has become a carmine red, the silvery starflower and the ivory-colored wintergreen have a rose cast. The flowers have become smaller too, but they are more fragrant than down in the forest. How many million acres of Norway's forests have come to an end under the cheese kettles at thousands of saeters it is impossible to say, but they have been costly to the country, these old-fashioned saeter practices. The old dairymaids can protest as much as they like that the old ways were more pleasant; from an economic point of view.

the modern arrangement with creameries in the valley is a step ahead.

Hanna still set aside *römmekoller*—shallow wooden bowls in which milk is allowed to sour and a thick layer of cream to form—for Sigurd had said that she must cook *römmegraut* for Sigrid and her boys once a week or so. The thick cream porridge is a favorite dish of all Norwegian children and Thursday was a red-letter day at Krekke saeter, for that evening Hanna treated everyone to *römmegraut*. Otherwise, the fare was rather dull. Hanna had three dishes to offer—dried ham and scrambled eggs, meat balls the farmer's wife had put up at the last slaughtering, and trout. But to Hans these were the very best things in the world.

The afternoon hours, from the time the dairy-maids finished with the cheese making and until the cows came home, the womenfolk at the saeter could take things quietly. They went visiting from saeter to saeter, having coffee together and talking, always with a piece of needlework in their hands. Mother also laid aside her writing and accompanied Hanna to Björge saeter, or down to the Prestang saeters, or over to Ledumssla, where Hanna's married sister took care of her own saeter and had all her children with her. Hans very much liked these afternoon coffee parties, for everyone served seven different sorts of cookies and cakes with the coffee, as well as freshly made waffles. And everywhere there was something new and interesting to see. At Ledumssla there were three sows, and two of them had each just had a litter of little pigs—and newborn pigs are the sweetest things in the world. Mrs. Ledum told a story about her neighbor, Per Brekkum, who had had two young actresses from Oslo staying at his saeter last summer, and these two from the city had become so enthralled with the sight of newborn pigs that they had shouted and shrieked and declared they had *never* seen anything so bewitching.

"Per, you surely won't drown them all, will you? You'll let the mother pig keep one or two, won't you?"

But it was not wholly unlikely, said Mrs. Ledum, chuckling, that Per had made up the story. He was fond of ridiculing city people. Several years ago he had taken in an unemployed person from Oslo who had come wandering up the road asking for work. Per had hired him as a dairyman. When evening came he handed the boy from Oslo a milk pail and a stool and sent him to the barn to milk the cows. After a long time, he came in, this city fellow, all dirty and perspiring and with black and blue marks on his face and arms.

"No, my good man," he had said to the farmer, "this

job is not for me, after all. I've been working with your blasted old cows out there for three hours now and I still haven't got one of them to sit down on the stool."

At least that was the story Per told.

On Björge saeter there was a wonderfully fine pair of binoculars. The owner's daughter, Magda, who was at the saeter as a dairymaid, stood in a gable window nearly all afternoon, watching a herd of elk that came down toward evening to graze on a grassy plot on the other side of Tromsa. There was a great bull with wide-spreading branched antlers, and three cows, each with a calf. Kongsparten this plain was called, and the strange thing about it was that every once in a while an air picture, or mirage, appeared above it: a picture of a harbor with fishing schooners and boats in it, with yellow and white boat sheds beside a pier and a white lighthouse against the blue water of the bay. Mother and Hans dropped in at Björge saeter rather often in order to look at the herd of elk through Magda's binoculars, in hopes of seeing the mirage. Mother fancied she would be able to recognize the harbor and say where on the coast it could be found. But she never had a chance, for the mirage never appeared while Mother and Hans were at Goppollen.

The men at Björge had been great hunters for generations. But now game was scarce in the mountains.

Nevertheless, Magnar was at the saeter with his dogs
He had an elkhound, champion in his class and the
winner of a whole shelfful of silver medals and blue
ribbons, and a young Irish setter, a red-haired beauty
who, though nervous and irritable, had accustomed
herself to Mother and Hans and was relatively friendly
toward them. Magnar was waiting for the hunting season to begin, but meanwhile he helped his sister with
a little of everything. Yes, there were attractions
enough at Björge saeter, besides the fact that the buildings there were the oldest and the handsomest of all
the saeters in Goppollen.

Hans quickly accustomed himself to hearing everyone up here call his mother by her first name and use
the familiar "du" to her. Soon he himself began calling
her Sigrid, not mother.

"For Sigrid's a rather pretty name, don't you think?"
he observed one day.

"Absolutely," Mother declared. "One of my grand-
mothers was named Algaard Kristine, and the other one
Clara Severine Petrea, so I consider myself lucky. My
father wanted me named for all my ancestral mothers
at Sollia and Österdalen and all these women were
named either Sigrid or Ingeborg, as far as I know."

Johanne never went to these coffee parties at the
other saeters. In her free time, she sat with a sketchbook

181

and colored crayons, drawing. When she and Mother
had become so well acquainted that Johanne could lay
aside her shyness, she confided to Mother that she was
going to be a painter. A sister of her father's was married to a doctor in Oslo and this aunt had promised
Johanne might live with them when she had finished
school. Then she was going to try to get into the Acad-
emy. And when she had learned enough so that she
could give an exhibition and perhaps get a grant, she
would live in Paris in winter and come home every
summer and be dairymaid at Goppollen. That was
what Miss Jahn did, the daughter of the pastor they
used to have in the parish. She was a painter and lived
abroad every winter and worked as dairymaid at home
every summer. This year she was at Nord-Elstad
saeter. That was one of the saeters where a light always
burned late in the evenings, there below the mountain
on the other side of Big Tromsa. For the most part
Johanne copied picture postcards and pictures from
magazines—some good, some bad. But when she took
her courage in her hands and tried to make sketches of
her own from things around her here in the mountains,
she was really good, especially in doing cows and
horses.

The doll house took up a great deal of Hans's and

Janna's time. It superseded even the little girl's knitting, and Hans disturbed his mother in her work all too
often with his demands that she help with this and help
with that. Their children, Jöda and Little Mari, went
on strike the second day.

"I only said it the way you say it to me," Hans related afterward. " 'I would rather not punish you, but
if you do that again I'll have to give you a spanking.' "

Little Mari became grossly offended. She refused,
straight out, to be Hans's child any longer. In fact, she
began to pout and said she didn't want to stay there
any longer . . . she wanted to go home to her mother.
And when her father, Sigurd Hole, arrived on Saturday evening, Little Mari demanded with great force
that he take her home with him Sunday. So as Sigurd
drove down to the valley, Little Mari sat on his lap, so
self-important that she did not even deign to wave to
Hans and Janna, though they shouted and called
"levvel," good-by, to her. But she merely pouted and
pretended she did not know them.

Nor did Jöda wish to play house any longer. All day
long she lay across the long dining table in the saeter
house, surrounded with paper bags from the store and
all the wrapping paper she could get her hands on,
making rough drafts in her large print of the letters she

was going to write to her grandmother in Lom and to her cousins in America. She had won a box of the loveliest writing paper at a bazaar. Some of the sheets were decorated with bouquets of roses, others with swallows carrying letters in their bills, some with two hands clasped in a garland of forget-me-nots. On the envelopes a grownup had written neatly and plainly the names and addresses of those for whom the letters were intended—Miss Loretta Hogan, 2121 East 78 St., Fargo, North Dakota, U.S.A., and Mrs. Jöda Haugen, Hole, Lesjaverk, Gudbrandsdalen.

Soon every time a wind played over the meadow it whirled around large pieces of gray wrapping paper inscribed with "My der cusin Loreta and Majori and cusin Kenet . . ." or "My good grandmother and name" . . .

"How well you write, Jöda, even though you are so little," declared Mother. "You haven't gone to school more than one year, have you?"

But Jöda had not even started school. Her grandmother had lived with them the preceding winter and she had taught Jöda to read the headlines in the newspapers and to print the letters.

Hans was so dejected because Jöda and Little Mari had deserted them.

"If only we had those dolls of Tulla's she doesn't

care about anyway," Hans reflected to Mother.
"Mother, can't you write to Thea and ask her to send
them to us?"

But that Mother could not do. It was true Tulla
never played with the two Käthe-Kollwitz dolls Mother
had once bought for her, but their place was the shelf
above her bed, and Tulla could not abide having any
thing changed in the rooms at home.

At last they found a solution. Mother selected from
the woodpile two nice sticks of birchwood with smooth
white bark. She borrowed Johanne's colored crayons
and drew faces on the bark. Then the sticks were
swathed in kerchiefs and Mother sacrificed a shoe box
to make a cradle. Now Hans and Janna had two sweet
little babies, and they were busy the livelong day changing the didies, and giving them the bottle, and now and
then, a wee bit of upbringing.

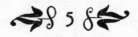

IT WAS GETTING ON TOWARD FALL. ONE NOTICES THE coming of fall earlier in the mountains than in the valley. The leaves on the blueberry bushes had a red cast, and the branches were heavy with dark, ripe berries. And everywhere on the marshes shone the cloudberries. These were still hard as stone and lacquer red.

In Norway people think there is nothing so good as cloudberries. Certainly the cloudberry is one of the most beautiful of plants. The big broad leaves are a deep, deep green with a tinge of bronze and violet in them, the flowers in the spring are white, and the berries before they ripen are like the round old-fashioned coral brooches. When at last the fruit turns soft and yellow gold it is ripe. It has a sharp, invigorating taste unlike any other taste in the world. Foreigners often find it too sharp.

In Eastern Norway all the great wastes in the high

est mountains and in the forests are adorned with cloudberry bogs. But it is not every year that people get enough cloudberries to talk about. A frost during the flowering season or early in the fall before the berries are ripe can ruin all the fruit.

This year promised to be the biggest cloudberry year anyone could remember. Thea wrote to Mother to buy as many berries as she could get hold of—a hundred quarts, if possible—for when properly put up they last for years.

The days were longer in the mountains under the high open dome of heaven than down in the village, but it was noticeable here too that the evenings came earlier every day. The nights were darker, and the wind that was always sighing and moaning out on the plain had an even more melancholy sound and felt chill. And the cows were getting to be a nuisance the way they did not come home until late.

The Krekke cows were still not too bad. They were not nearly so troll-like as the Prestang cows, not to mention Ingrid's cows at Nyplass saeter. Ingrid was an elderly widow who cared for her own saeter. She had only four cows, some calves, and a small herd of goats. And Ingrid's cows would never come home by themselves. Every evening the people at Krekke saw the old woman set out for the ford beyond Björge, knitting as she walked. She was going to the other side of the river to look for her cows. She would have to clamber up and down all the bluffs and search every valley. It would often be pitch-dark before they heard her bringing home her cows.

And now Hanna's cows had begun to be a bother. There were so many mushrooms in the woods now, and cows are quite mad about mushrooms. They traveled far down in the wood to get them and ate and ate and could never stop. Often the early fall dark had fallen before they came home—and by the time Hanna and Johanne had got them all in their stalls and given them the evening feeding of warm mash made of chopped straw and meal and salt that all saeter cows get, it was almost night.

Janna had to come and help with the milking, little as she was, for they were milking eighteen cows at Krekke saeter. Mother, too, put on an old blue house dress, tied a kerchief over her hair, and went down to the barn.

Never had Hans been so impressed by his mother as that day he discovered she could milk a cow.

"But—but—you say you are afraid of cows, Mother!"

"I am—of cows I don't know personally."

"But, Mother, where did you learn how to milk?"

188

"In the country on summer vacations, when I was a little girl. But, Hans, don't stand there right in the doorway, like that."

He was in the way of the milkmaids as they went to empty their pails in the big milk can outside the door. Besides, cows do not like having strangers around in the barn when they are being milked.

But Hans could not tear himself away. There is nothing so pleasant as an old saeter barn such as this one on an autumn night, when the weather is raw and windy. Here inside was a good, living warmth from the heavy bodies of cows, and the two little lanterns, hanging from the ridgepole, threw a gentle, golden glow into the dim, velvety-brown interior. For the Krekke barn was very old. The date 1792 was carved in a log in the wall. The ceiling was low and the stalls, with flagstones set on edge for partitions, were small, but it seemed that the cows found it just as pleasant here as in the big, airy barn down on the farm, where Sigurd Hole had installed all kinds of improvements and modern equipment. Their very breathing sounded like sighs of content and well-being as they gulped down their warm evening mash. Then they chewed their cuds, stamping their feet a little, and occasionally switched their tails in the faces of the persons milking them. And above all these peaceful sounds came the rhythmic ring of the milk streaming and foaming into the buckets.

Then Hanna lighted the little kerosene lamp in the saeter house and hung it up over the long dining table. Mother was so much at home in the house now that she could set out the evening meal for herself and Hans while Hanna and Johanne strained the milk and turned the separator. The separator's rhythmic hum filled the room as Hans and Mother ate, and out of the night from far and near came the hum of other separators on other saeters. When they had finished, Hanna and Johanne came and sat down at the table too. True enough, they had had their supper while they waited for the cows, but another cup of coffee and slice of bread wouldn't hurt. . . .

Mother had hung aside her milking costume and scrubbed thoroughly as soon as she came in from the milking. Nevertheless, Hans sniffed of her as she bathed him and put him to bed.

"Gee, Mother, you smell so nice." He sighed ecstatically and pressed against her. "You smell exactly like a peasant woman."

But Anders burst into a loud guffaw the evening he suddenly bobbed up beneath the lantern in the doorway of the barn.

"Why, if it isn't— God save my soul! If you **aren't** playing at the milkmaid up here, Mother!"

He was carrying a full pack—a knapsack, a fishing rod in a sailcloth case, and a pair of high rubber boots dangling beside the knapsack.

"I didn't see any light and I couldn't imagine what had become of you. Hello, Hans. Are you making yourself useful too? Perhaps my brother cleans the barn . . . ?"

"Go down to the house and sit down," Mother said unconcernedly. "We'll fix you something to eat when we finish here. Where did you come from, by the way?"

Anders said he had been home several days.

"I'm to greet you for them all. . . . Yes, everything is fine."

He had come by train to Losna station that morning and walked up the old footpath to the saeter.

"It's much shorter than the road, but it's steep, of course. And the lemmings up here! Phew! I've seen so many lemmings in these mountains, you can't imagine!"

Yes, whenever Mother and Hans went walking they saw lemmings everywhere. Actually, lemmings are dainty little animals with fine, silky, yellow- and brown-flecked fur and white bellies. But their bodies are flat and broad, reminding one inevitably of bedbugs. And in the exact center of the face is that typical rodent's mouth with sharp, protruding teeth. They have vicious dispositions, these little animals, and stand barking and sputtering and squeaking shrilly at whoever comes upon them.

Hans used to take a stick and tease them.

"Mother, they say a lemming gets so angry he bursts if you keep on pricking him long enough."

"But don't do that, Hans. I don't know if it is true, but leave them in peace. Poor things, they'll all come to an end, one way or the other, before winter sets in."

Mother moved her toilet articles into her study and turned the back room over to the boys. Anders emptied out the contents of his knapsack and by the time the brothers were ready to go to bed the room was as disorderly and bedraggled as their room at home.

Mother and Anders lay sunning themselves on the grass of the little slope next morning and Anders was telling about his hiking trip with Godfather and Uncle George. It was astonishing how big and mature the boy had become in these few weeks. His body was tough and wiry, and his face was burned a mahogany brown. Actually, his eyes were gray-green, but they were so dark when he became excited or eager about something that they seemed to be coal black.

They had hiked through the mountains north of Jotunheimen, away from the usual tourist trails. They had slept in stone huts and fished in waters that did not even appear on the map.

"Kristians Amt, Northern Part," said Mother, laughing. "I know it very well, thank you. That map was already old when I was a young girl and went hiking in those mountains. But now the General Staff has promised to issue a new relief map of Loms Mountains next year."

Anders nodded.

"But it was fun, just the same, to be in mountains so poorly charted. It was always like being on an exploring expedition in virgin territory."

They had hiked over to Drivdalen and then proceeded on down into Sollia.

"You can't imagine what nice people live around there, Mother. Especially when they heard I was your son. You must be related to every single soul in the valley, aren't you?"

"I'm sure of it," said Mother. "You know Sollia was a saeter mountain until about 1650 when the first colony of people came up and cleared some land for themselves to see if they could live there the year around. There were five families from Österdalen and every-

HAPPY TIMES IN NORWAY

one in Sollia to this day is descended from one of them."

"The mayor told me to remember him to you and to tell you that you should sell your house and buy a place in Sollia. Taxes are low there so you could save a lot of money if you moved back there."

"What about a school for you? There is certainly nothing but a grammar school in Sollia. I would have to send you away from home to live with strangers the whole school year."

"You know I could live with Captain Dahl," said Anders. "They take school children to room and board. Sheriff Gunstad's daughters from Ringbu live there."

Suddenly he blushed scarlet.

Mother pretended not to notice.

"From Sollia," Anders then went on, "we walked back over the Ringbu Mountains. Some people from Sollia came with us . . . and we went over to Snödöla and took a look at the ruins of that stone hut where people of Sollia surrounded that runaway, Kristen, and killed him. Mother, you are a descendant of Gypsy Kristen too."

"So I am," said Mother shortly.

"So there is gypsy blood in you—and in us children?" Anders asked excitedly.

"Not at all. We are descended from one of his daughters by his wife, Sigrid Sollia. No one knows whether he had any children by the gypsy girl, and if he did, certainly no one asked about them. Heavens, child, don't get the idea that Gypsy Kristen was anyone romantic or great. A peasant who deserted his farm, and his wife and children, for the sake of a gypsy girl and who joined a bunch of hoodlums and went stealing and plundering on all the farms of his old neighbors. He was nothing but a renegade! He got only what he deserved when the people of Sollia killed him over there in Snödöl Valley."

"Perhaps so. I didn't think of that. But, Mother, I heard another story over there about another ancestor of yours—Anders Grötdalen."

"He was my grandfather's grandfather."

Mother knew the story, but she sensed Anders was dying to tell it.

THEY WERE STAYING AT GRÖTDAL SAETER, ANDERS and his cousin, Halvor Tangen, and one day the cows came tearing home, gone completely wild. This was a sure sign that a bear was around. Halvor took his musket and both fellows started out. They found the bear. He had brought down a heifer and she was still alive and a horrible sight. The bear started for them and before they knew it Anders Grötdalen was behind a large old fir tree and had the bear by both forepaws. The bear was on the other side of the tree, snapping to right and left, but without reaching Anders and hurting him.

"Well, you've got such a good hold on him," Halvor Tangen said, "you can probably hold him while I run home to the saeter and get the ax. That way we'll save a bullet."

So Anders stood and held the bear by the forelegs until the Tangen boy went to the saeter and came back again with the ax.

"Say, that was my heifer," Anders said then, "so it's only right that you let me kill the beast."

Halvor agreed to this. He took Anders's place back of the spruce tree, and got hold of the bear's forelegs. Anders then took the ax.

But then Anders said, "Say, I'm awful hungry. I'd like to go down to the saeter first and get me a bite to eat. You can probably hold him that long."

With that Anders ran away and left Halvor holding the bear. He did not come back until he had been gone exactly as long as Halvor had stayed. Then he bashed in the head of the bear. They said the old bearskin that hangs in Sollia chapel is the hide of this bear. At least it is moth-eaten and old enough to be.

"Have you ever heard that story before, mother?"

"Oh, I heard it some time or the other, when I was little. Ingebrikt, the hired man at my grandfather's, belonged to the family too, and he liked to tell about the old folks of Sollia—just so Grandfather did not hear him. Grandfather was a very religious man, you know. He had been converted while he was away at military service. After that he did not like to hear much talk about the people of Sollia. They were a wild lot, you know, most of them, and this Halvor Tangen—Tang-gutten, they called him—was one of the worst."

"If I were you, I still think I would consider it— moving back to Sollia, I mean," Anders declared.

Mother shook her head.

"It's almost a hundred years since Grandfather left Sollia. He was only two when his father died, and his mother took him home with her to her parents in Öster-dalen. And when he grew up he came to Trondheim. Since then none of us have been farmers. We would not be of much use in the mountains."

"But they were fine people, just the same. It's fun to think of our being descended from those fellows."

"Yes, it is. And we'll have to try to be a credit to the people of Sollia—do what we have to do wherever we may be placed in the world as well as they did in Sollia."

THERE WAS NOT MUCH FOR MOTHER AND ANDERS TO
talk about these days. Every morning after breakfast
he took his fishing outfit and went down to Tromsa.
But his luck was not good. Sometimes he came home
empty-handed, sometimes with one or two tiny trout
in his pocket. Ingrid's cat got them. He rarely caught
any fish big enough to be worth the trouble of cleaning and frying. Tromsa was not good fishing, and
Anders, apparently, was not much of a fisherman.

Once in a while he went berrypicking with the other
children. Blueberries were incredibly thick this year
and the cloudberries were ripening enough so a few of
them could be picked too. But truth to tell, it was not
especially interesting for Anders up here. He had no
one to keep him company, and it was not his bent to
busy himself with anything about the saeter.

Sigurd Hole came up with two men to cut the hay

SUMMER VACATION

Nothing smells so sweet as the hay from these mountain meadows, but it is a little sad to see the flower-spangled grass fall before the scythe. Then one knows for certain it is fall. Anders borrowed a scythe and started cutting too, but he soon gave up. He was clumsy that way. His idea of becoming a farmer at Sollia was indeed a transient dream. But Hans and the little girls busied themselves with the raking and helped to hang the hay on the drying rack—taking care to follow the haying crew indoors each time one of the customary extra meals for haymakers was to be served.

But Anders was pleasant toward everyone, not even teasing his brother about playing with a little girl in a doll house. Hans had expected his brother to tease him about that and had been prepared to tease Anders all he could in turn. But the boys were the best friends in the world up here.

A boy of fourteen is very much older than he was when he was thirteen, thought Mother. And one fine afternoon, as Anders sat with her out on the lawn, he drew a long and fervent sigh.

"It isn't going to be half bad to get back to school again—oh, as far as that goes," he added quickly and politely, "it is very nice up here and, all in all, it has been a fine summer vacation. But after a while one gets tired of never having anything to do."

One felt chill now in the morning. The heavens were a deep, brilliant blue and the air so clear that to the north one could see the snow mountains, with all their peaks and gorges, outlined sharply against the horizon. In summer one only suspected something dazzlingly bright over there where the clouds hovered above the melting snow fields. And one morning the high gray peaks that formed the Österdalen boundary were white far down the sides with newly fallen snow.

Anders had even bought and brought with him a birthday present for Hans—a knife. The boys always got a great assortment of knives for Christmas and on their birthdays and it was inconceivable what became of them all, but they were always coming to Mother to "borrow" a knife. When Hans's birthday came, Anders, however, could not remember what he had done with the gift for his brother. Both boys spent all morning looking through Anders's pockets and his knapsack and all his fishing things. By the time they finally found the knife—on the floor under Anders's bed—the car with the company from home was already in the yard.

First both the dogs tumbled out. Njord leaped on Mother and licked her face so enthusiastically that he scratched her lip and made it bleed. Neri whizzed

about so happy to see his family again that he did not
know what to do with himself. Jöda and Janna were
terrified by these wild, coal-black dogs and ran indoors.
But Johanne coaxed the dogs over to her and succeeded
in petting them.

"Say, what two nice pooches you got here, Sigrid!
What life in them!" she said, addressing Mother, as
usual, with "du."

Tulla seemed to be just as happy as the dogs, though
in a slightly more subdued manner. She would not let
go of Mother's hand for anything, and she called to
Hans and Anders constantly, laughing delightedly.
Thea had brought a reclining chair, which she now
set up against the sunny wall of the *lunnbu*, and put
Tulla into it, a pillow under her head and a cover across
her legs. Tulla should take a little nap now, Thea said,
for they had been driving since early morning. Hans
was to have his hot chocolate and his birthday cake—
the twisted yeast ring with raisins in it and sugar and
almonds on top—at twelve o'clock, and before the company left he would have the usual birthday dinner
with all the things to eat that he always had on his
birthday. Thea and Böe were busy carrying all the
baskets and cakeboxes down to the saeter house.

The boys raced around their grandmother explaining the names of all the mountains that could be seen

from the yard. Little Signe had discovered in the goat shed two lovely little newborn kids, snow white. Unfortunately, Njord also had discovered them. Little Signe grabbed him by the chops and got him out in a hurry. Then she locked herself in with the baby kids. . . .

Now came Thea calling that the chocolate was ready.

Hanna had decorated the saeter house so prettily, strewing fresh juniper on the floor and setting vases of mountain flowers—buttercups and shooting stars and the blue monkshood—on the table. She stood by the stove making cream waffles and the whole yard smelled of them. Thea lighted the eight candles on the birthday ring and poured the chocolate into the cups, and Hanna appeared with a huge bowl of whipped cream stiff enough to cut with a knife.

All the children ate and drank as if they had not eaten for a week, though Johanne was chiefly occupied with the dogs. It was a disgrace the way they stood beside her, their forepaws in her lap, begging waffles. Janna sat tenderly fingering the paper napkins Thea had brought along. They looked exactly like real napkins and had checked borders in many colors.

It was impossible for Mother to get to talk with Grandmother. There were so many things the boys simply had to show her. Anders thought Grandmother should certainly come with them to see the pond where the golden plover's nest had been that summer.

"It's so beautiful there, grandmother. The water is so blue now you can't believe your eyes, and there is a floating island with some little birches on it that look exactly like lighted candles with their yellow leaves. It's just up the hill there, and beyond that little cliff you see over there . . ."

But just as they reached the top of the hill and saw the little pond, like a blue eye right below them, Grandmother shrieked in terror.

"Oh, good heavens, there are bulls down there!"

Grandmother was deathly afraid of animals. She dared not even walk past a month-old calf. And down by the edge of the pond there were actually four pretty little bull calves.

Anders pulled up a dry juniper root and ran down to drive them away.

"Oh, God!" Grandmother shook with fear. "Sigrid, get that boy to come back. Oh, God, what if they gore him to death! Anders, Anders, come here," she called miserably after him.

Hans and Little Signe tried to reassure her, but they were laughing so hard they finally had to roll in the heather.

"Why, Grandmother, they're only calves."

But Grandmother did not want to stay any longer "in these wild mountains where you run the risk of meeting all kinds of dangerous animals walking around loose." She wanted to go back down the hill to the security of the saeter fence. In great annoyance she turned her back on the children and started down the path with quick, determined steps. Mother followed, and behind came Anders, who grasped Mother's arm and silently pointed.

Mother had already seen them. Down the road came a herd of bulls—at least twelve of them. Most of them were young bulls but there were several big ones among them, and one was a light-gray color. In Hadlands-legeret, a valley between the gray mountains toward Österdalen, a herd of a hundred bulls was quartered—animals that would be sold for beef in the fall. Now that the feed had become scarce, an occasional herd would sometimes travel as far as Krekke during the course of the day. And among them there was supposed to be a big gray bull not to be trusted.

"Mean, did you say?" the herder at Hadland had asked. "No, he's not mean. Of course he sometimes tosses a stranger on his horns."

"By the way, grandmother," Anders said, "we *must* stop in at Ingrid's saeter. She has a cat that is a son of that daughter of Sissi at Thorstad. He is *so* pretty grandmother, you *must* see him . . . such fine long fur . . . dark brown with yellow spots . . ."

And Anders took his grandmother by the arm and steered her hurriedly north toward the nearest saeter Hans and Little Signe had already started running to ward Nyplass. Fortunately, they had not noticed the bulls up on the road.

Anders chattered and chattered, pointed, gesticulated, and gestured at such a rate that Grandmother did not have a chance to turn around once before she was well inside the fence enclosing Ingrid's hayfield. Even then this reticent, taciturn boy continued to preach and point out so many curious, remarkable things on this poor little saeter of Ingrid's that Mother thought Grandmother must surely suspect something. The cat came right over to Anders, for it had got all those little fish from him, and he presented it to Grandmother, conducting a lecture at the same time on its family history and recalling other offspring of Sissi. Then he related all Ingrid's troubles with the cows that never came home by themselves, and this got Grandmother and Ingrid involved in a long conversation.

Luckily none of the bulls bellowed as they passed Ingrid's gate, and Grandmother did not notice a thing Not until the animals were only little specks far out on the moor did Anders give the sign to say good-by to Ingrid and go home.

"Poor thing, she would have had a stroke at least, if we had met them," whispered Anders to Mother. "And she would certainly never let Little Signe stay on up here awhile."

Thea had warmed up the baked chicken stuffed with rice and mushrooms she had brought along and, for dessert, Hanna brought out cloudberries and cream. Thea had brought canned pineapple along for dessert and Janna and Jöda thought they had never tasted anything so good as pineapple. Country people cannot afford American canned fruit, whereas they could have cloudberries at home every Sunday—if it was a good year for cloudberries. And when Janna and Jöda also got all the leftover paper napkins, Hans's birthday became for them also a glorious feast day.

Little Signe was to stay a week or so with her aunt. But Anders packed his things and said he wished to go home in the car this evening.

"You see, mother, there is always a thing or two to do before school starts—get out the books, take a look at the Scout lodge, and so on."

Yes, Mother understood.

It was hard to say good-by to Tulla. She was sad when she realized that Mother was not going to ride with them in the car. But it comforted her a little when Anders sat down beside her and put his arm around her shoulders.

"Mother's coming soon, Tulla. Mother has only to finish something she's working on up here, and then she will come home to you."

Ah, yes, it was a good thing Anders went back with them to town.

LITTLE SIGNE'S STAY AT KREKKE SAETER TURNED OUT to be a great disappointment to Hans. She was not one bit impressed by the doll house. On the contrary, she made several rather unkind remarks about its past—a past that could not be concealed.

On the other hand, she became utterly infatuated with Janna's sweater, which now had actually begun to take on lines that were rather stunning. The frank admiration of this little town girl was so stimulating to Janna that she would scarcely do anything but knit, knit, knit all day long.

"Oh dear," said Little Signe, "how I wish I had some knitting."

Mother said she had a sweater she rarely used, for she did not like it. It was made of variegated yarn—pink and gray and blue—and it could be unraveled.

"Oh, that'll make enough yarn for a sweater for me," cried Little Signe. "I'm so little compared to you."

"You can't knit a sweater," declared Mother. "Remember Janna is more than two years older than you. You had better knit just a scarf, and maybe a ski cap."

But Little Signe so wanted to try knitting a sweater. Mother finally had to cast on the stitches and start the border for her.

From that moment on, the two little girls sat on the bench outside the door and knitted all day long. Mother, watching them, did not see them exchange a word except when they held up their knitting to show how much they had done. Little Signe did not do at all badly. When that youngster made up her mind to do something she nearly always managed to do it.

"From now on," declared Hans in disgust, "Ulla is going to be my favorite cousin."

He consoled himself, however, with visits to the cat at Nyplass saeter, and soon he was firmly ensconced at Ingrid's. Mother saw him there whenever she went walking that way. Hans carried in water and carried in wood, and obviously he was a bosom friend of that old widow whom everybody considered "difficult." That meant she was well-nigh impossible to get along with, but people here in the valley never used strong words to express disapproval of any of their neighbors.

"It's going to storm tonight," Hanna said one afternoon as she stood kneading the cheese. There was a thunder of hoofs on the road as a herd of horses came galloping down toward the saeters. And when horses that run loose in the mountains do that, it is a sure sign of a coming storm. Out on the plain from every direction came lowing and bellowing and a strange hush hung in the air.

"I'll have to go for the cows today, I think," Hanna said and threw her knitted shawl over her head.

In weather such as this the cows might come home earlier than usual by themselves, but if the storm broke while they were deep in the mountains they would be just as likely to seek shelter under a crag up there and be out all night. Milkmaids from all the saeters began to appear on the road. They had all had the same thought.

"Come on, come o-on, come o-o-on . . ." came their call from all sides.

The mountains to the north were lost in masses of dark clouds. The sunlight fell across the meadow dazzlingly yellow and all the colors out on the table-land became sharp and bright and clear. The green dwarf willow on the bogs turned bright green, and the red dwarf birch were pools of blood.

"Just so the cloudberries don't get ruined," sighed Johanne. Then, "We'd better take in the wash."

The first burst came as they were busy out by the clothesline. The sheet Johanne and Mother stood folding was torn from their fingers and went sailing far through the air before drifting down north of the hayfield. Aprons and cotton house dresses stood straight out from the line, or wrapped themselves tightly around it. Janna and Hans chased fugitive garments all over the field, and almost got blown away themselves. Before they had got in the last clothesbasketful, rain was spurting down from the skies and splashing up from the ground.

The slope between the saeter house and the *lunnbu* was a tearing stream when Mother and the children ran up from the house in the pitch-dark after they had eaten supper. Before they got through their doorway they were wet as drowned cats, all three. And the *lunnbu* was full of sour, acrid smoke that made their eyes smart. Chimneys smoked in such weather.

Mother had to rake out the coals from both stoves. Sparks and burning bits of wood flew out and burned holes in her apron while Hans and Little Signe had a busy time stamping out the sparks scattered over the floor.

The children had to be content this evening with a mere "cat wash" of their faces. The chimney howled and, outside, the wind roared and moaned around the corners of the house, and on the roof something was rattling terrifically.

"It's only that galvanized iron Sigurd patched the roof with," Mother said reassuringly.

Little Signe was plainly terrified, though she tried hard not to show it.

"It would probably be best if you both slept with me tonight," said Mother. "There is not quite so much smoke there as out here."

It was rather crowded sleeping three in a bed. Especially since Hans curled up in such a fashion that he took up nearly all the room. He slept like a rock all night, and did not even feel it when Mother tried to straighten him out and shove him against the wall. But Little Signe awakened every other minute.

"Aunt," she whispered tensely, "what's that?"

There was a terrific clatter and racket right outside.

"Just a chunk of wood that rolled down the woodpile. Lie down and go to sleep now."

"Aunt, it's blowing so hard. Aunt, the roof couldn't blow off, could it?"

"Of course not, Signe. It'll stay on all right. Go to sleep now."

"Aunt, what is *that?*"

Something bumped against the wall on the other side of the bed—then bumped and thudded and bumped again. Then came a bellow—loud and penetrating.

"Bulls. Some must have tried to find shelter from the storm here by the north wall."

"Aunt, do you think they could butt in the wall and come in here where we are?"

"No, no. You don't have to be afraid. Now my little girl must try to go to sleep. It's awful weather tonight—but those of us who are lying abed indoors, all warm and safe and sound—we're lucky, aren't we, Signe?"

Toward morning the wind subsided a little. When Mother and the children came out, a thick mist lay over the world. Pressed close against the north wall of the *lunnbu* stood four strange young bulls, so wet that their red hides looked black as coal. And on the woodpile lay the doll house on its side, and all Janna's pretty cards and paper napkins were pulp. Their pretty little doll dishes floated in water and the boards that had hidden the holes lay floating in a pond some distance away.

Janna and Hans and Little Signe stood, gunny sacks over their heads, surveying the monstrous destruction. They had not cared a great deal for their doll house recently—at least they had not played in it so much—but now they were desolate at its having come to such a sorrowful end. Even Little Signe, who had been so scorn-

ful of it when she had first been invited to come and
play in it, was sorry.

"And it was so lo-ve-ly. Oh, what a shame!"

She picked up the two poor wooden dolls.

"Aunt, if we dry them, don't you think you could
draw faces on them again? They were so sweet."

Janna said not a word. Norwegian children are early
taught self-control. It is a disgrace to cry "if there is
nothing worth while to cry about." And country people
are especially stern with their children in this matter.
Janna's bright little face was strained and tense as she
struggled to hold back the tears.

Mother had received a number of picture postcards
during the course of the summer, along with all the
other mail that came to her by car on Saturday, and it
comforted Janna somewhat when Mother presented
her with these, though most of these postcards were
photographs, and Janna's cards had been such elegant
ones, all colored and gilded and glazed.

But Little Signe promised to send her some colored
picture postcards from Oslo and Mother promised to
find some cards with glaze on them when she got back
to town. And then it helped some that she still had all
those paper napkins left over from Hans's birthday.

The wooden dolls were bundled up in shawls that
had been warmed by the stove, and tucked into a new

cradle made from another empty box. Then they were
fed warm milk and given aspirin. Little by little the
children forgot their sorrow as they busied themselves
in Mother's house, doctoring and nursing their two
little patients. By afternoon the babies were so much
better that they could be sent over to Mother, who had
just opened a beauty parlor, and who gave them a facial
with red and blue and yellow crayons.

The stormy weather lasted three days. On the fourth
morning the sun shone from a cloudless, dark-blue sky.
But the golden birch groves were now naked and
brown, and the glorious colors on the tableland had
faded. All was sere and brown and a graying yellow
now.

Hanna and Mother and all the children went for a
walk to the nearest cloudberry bog. Fortunately, the
cloudberries had not been too ripe or they would have
been ruined. But it was high time the cloudberry pickers turned up, if they were going to collect all this
wealth before autumn came in earnest and spoiled
everything.

Next day between sixty and seventy trucks appeared,
loaded with tubs, pails, buckets, bedding and lunch
baskets, and parked along the saeter road from Nyplass
to Björge saeter. Every saeter house became filled with

berrypickers, or berryhunters, as they were called here in the valley, sleeping four or five in a bed, and in rows on the floor. Other berrypickers lay in tents and on the ground in sleeping bags, and every evening after dark campfires appeared over all the plain. No one could remember there ever having been such a cloudberry year as this one. It would surely pay to lay in as big a supply as possible.

This was not the time to talk of being crowded when Little Signe and Hans and Mother had slept three in a bed the night of the big storm! Now Hanna and Mother and two women from down the valley all slept in Mother's bed, and in both beds in the back room children and young girls lay packed as tight as sardines, for the saeter house was as full of men as there was room for in the beds and on the floors. During the day everyone was out picking berries, filling their pails and then coming to empty them in kegs and barrels. Evenings, when it had become too dark for the pickers to see the berries, the air in the saeter house was so thick with the odor of greased leather boots, of clothes soaked through with rank swamp water, of perspiring bodies and of woodsmoke, and the smell of coffee and boiled milk that one could cut it with a knife. But it was a tremendous lot of fun to be in the midst of such feverish activity.

There was a telephone on Ledumssla saeter and every evening after dark people flocked down there. And the news from the valley was good—the fruit buyers were offering quite good prices, considering all the cloudberries there were this year, not only in these mountains, but all over Eastern Norway. Everyone was pleased—including Mother, who had managed to get two hundred quarts at a reasonable price. That was enough to last three years, even after sending some to her sisters and friends and acquaintances.

Then, one fine day, it was over, and the caravan of trucks, loaded high with buckets and barrels, and topped with happy people, started moving toward town. A few cloudberries naturally remained—enough for people on the saeters to have cloudberries for dessert every day, but the mountains had been so thoroughly gone over that it did not pay for anyone to pick for cash.

Little Signe sat enthroned on Sigurd Hole's lap, atop a cloudberry car. She had to leave now, for Grandmother wanted to take her back to Oslo with her when she went.

Hans's mouth dropped sadly as he said good-by to his formerly favorite cousin. He looked as if he would have cried—if it were not shameful to cry. . . .

"But, for heaven's sake," said Mother, "you were

hardly together, you two, anyway, while she was here."

"That's just it," complained Hans. "She didn't care about me at all, but just wanted to sit and knit with Janna. And we had always been best friends before. Now in a week you and I have to go down too—and then I have to start that *nasty* school . . ."

Hans turned and ran quickly into the *lunnbu*. Mother discreetly followed Hanna to the saeter house. Hans, it seemed, needed to be alone to get over his sadness that summer was over.

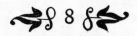

ONE DAY MRS. HOLE CAME UP TO SEE HER SAETER AND
she was almost like a summer guest herself. For when
a farmer engages a dairywoman for the summer, she
takes full responsibility and has full authority over
everything concerning the saeter, and it would be the
peak of bad manners if the farmer's wife allowed herself to interfere in any of the dairywoman's work.

Besides, Mrs. Hole probably needed a little vacation. Her husband had been building and fixing a little
of everything around on the farm down in the valley
this year, breaking and draining new ground too, so
Mrs. Hole had had as many as twenty men to board for
months at a time. She richly deserved a week's rest and
to be waited on and be cared for by Hanna.

She was called Janna, like her daughter, and Janna
Hole and Mother took many pleasant little walks together to the neighboring saeters and up the near-by

hills. Then one morning Mrs. Hole suggested they climb Hogtinden—there was a fine view from up there, and today the weather was so remarkably clear.

They equipped themselves with lunch and coffee-pot, and each slung a sack over her shoulder, for they would have to gather wood along the way. There was only gray moss and stone atop Hogtinden. When they set out they were quite alone, but before long the whole flock of youngsters was at their heels.

"Can't we be allowed to come too?"

The next one to join the company was that fine Irish setter from Björge saeter. Magda, carrying a large knapsack, and Magnar, with the binoculars slung over his shoulder, followed.

"We saw you start, so we got the idea of going up too."

The path ascends in zigzag, and the rise is so gradual one does not realize how high Hogtinden is until one climbs it. Janna Hole and Mother became quite tired and short of breath. They had to rest when they were halfway. That was on the very edge of the precipice where the snow owls had hatched their broods.

"See the falcon!" cried all the children to their mothers. Its reddish-brown wings shone in the sun as it hung motionless high in the blue heaven.

Meantime people were bobbing up along the path

from every which way. Someone at every saeter had seen people starting up the mountain and so had wanted to go up too.

"Why, if Ingrid isn't even staggering along," laughed Magnar. "Poor thing, do you think she'll make it?"

"Make it?" said his sister. "No one has been in the training this summer that Ingrid has. She'll pass us all, see if she doesn't."

And Ingrid did.

Finally they reached the utmost ridge. The wind blew cold and refreshingly on their hot, perspiring faces. And there, twenty or thirty yards away, rose the cairn of stones that marked the summit of Hogtinden.

Magnar found a place sheltered from the wind and started the fire. Magda got out the coffeepot and set it into the flames, bracing it with stones, and began unpacking her knapsack.

"Here are some meat balls," she said. "But it's a shame to offer these to you, Janna. They're not half so good as yours."

Actually these meat balls were made from the same recipe, for Mrs. Björge and Mrs. Hole were sisters. And they smelled delicious as Magda started them heating in a pan.

It had turned out to be quite a gathering around the

cairn. Fortunately, several others had also brought coffeepots and had gathered wood along the way.

Mountains without end spread out below them, monotonously green-brown and gray, scarred here and there with purpling clefts where a valley ran down, its sides laden with dark conifers. And everywhere water blinked bluely beneath the darker blue autumn sky from hundreds of little lakes and tarns that were joined by sparkling bands of stream and brook.

Lonely saeter groups, the little houses looking like gray rocks on the green saeter fields, broke the wilderness. To the south the land fell slowly down toward the larger communities and disappeared in a bluish haze; but to the north and west and east stood stark, high, naked mountains, the summits swathed in snow and the sides gray with rockfall.

The children swarmed around Magnar, wanting to borrow the binoculars, but Janna Hole and Mother lay flat on their backs on the moss carpet, resting.

"Yes, that high snow mountain to the northeast ought to be Solntoppene," declared Magnar. "That's way over on the Swedish border. Say, look at that," he shouted suddenly, and handed Mother the binoculars. "Wild reindeer. See them?"

In the old days these mountains were the home of great reindeer herds. Krag-Jörgensen rifles, increased

mountain travel, and finally the automobile roads had
almost rendered them extinct. A few years' protection,
however, had increased their number again. Now once
more one frequently saw little herds of wild reindeer.

An old fellow, called Paal, came over and pointed:

"You see that big pile of stones over there on the
other side of Djupsjön, on that little hill right east of
the lake? Yeah, it looks like a wart. Well, that's that
there Böral Tautrom." Paal chuckled.

There was a story about that cairn. Everyone knew
it, but Paal told it just the same. . . .

IN THE OLDEN DAYS, THIRTY YEARS AGO MAYBE, THE
peasants still used to take their own stuff to Oslo, or
Kristiania, as the town was called then. They set out
when the winter sledding started, long trainloads of
them, their sleds heaped high with meat and potatoes
and hides and tallow and whatever else they had to sell.
They figured it was cheaper than using the railroad
Besides this way they got a trip to town, for the dealers
they did business with always had a *bondestue,* a place
where the peasants could stay, free of charge, as long as
they liked. These lodgings did not amount to much—
only one single room with several tiers of bunks along
the walls. The peasants brought their own bedding and
food.

Well, one year soon after New Year, one letter after another began coming to the farmer, "Mr. Böral Tautrom." The letters were bills for coffee and groceries, a mowing machine, a sewing machine, seed grain and fertilizer. Some scalawag or other had bought all these things in Kristiania and charged them to "Böral Tautrom." These city people, you see, thought *that* sounded like some fine, old name from up the valley. No, they never caught the fellow. Oh, sure, people had their own ideas about who he was, but no one felt like getting mixed up in the affair. Besides, he wasn't from this neighborhood. He was from Oyer, people said . . .

Everyone laughed at the old story.

"Well, nowadays no one would do anything like that. It wasn't *exactly* honest, but those days the buyers cheated the farmers every chance they got. Oh, not all of them, of course, but *some* didn't think anything of cheating some dumb farmer. So some of us figured we ought to get even when we could. But, of course, it's not like that any more, no, not like that at all," Paal concluded:

Hans came over and lay down beside Mother and gazed out over the mountains below.

"Oh, Mother, if only we could stay here for always,"

---

he said fervently. But he had his mouth full of cold buttered waffle, and waffles in both hands, so his words did not have quite the moving effect they should

But he said it again that evening, as Mother was putting their freshly ironed clothes down in the suitcases.

"You can wait and change when we get home, Hans. Dirty clothes take such a lot of room. And it will be just until tomorrow."

"I wish we *never* had to go away from here, mother. I wish we could stay in the mountains forever."

"Oh, Hans, things aren't so bad as all that at home. Don't you think it might even be pleasant to get home —meet all your friends? And Tulla—"

"Yes-s. But then I have to go to school again. Darn that old school!"

"We have all had to go to school sometime, Hans. You too must learn something. And time goes so fast, once you get started. Before you know it'll be potato-digging vacation."

"Phew on potato-digging vacation," Hans snorted. "It always rains."

"Yes, but then it isn't long until Christmas. You surely like Christmas, don't you?"

"Yes-s, but it's pretty long until then," sighed Hans.

He was only half-consoled for having to leave the saeter and go home.

A NOTE ON THE TYPE

The text of this book is set on the Linotype in Fairfield, the first type-face from the hand of the distinguished American artist and engraver Rudolph Ruzicka. In its structure Fairfield displays the sober and sane qualities of a master craftsman whose talent has long been dedicated to clarity. It is this trait that accounts for the trim grace and virility, the spirited design and sensitive balance of this original type face.

Rudolph Ruzicka—who was born in Bohemia in 1883 and came to America in 1894—set up his own shop devoted to wood-engraving and printing in New York in 1913, after a varied career as a wood-engraver, in photoengraving and bank-note printing plants, as art-director and free-lance artist. He now lives and works at his home and studio in Dobbs Ferry, New York. He has designed and illustrated many books and has created a considerable list of individual prints—wood-engravings, line-engravings on copper, aquatints. W. A. Dwiggins wrote recently: "Until you see the things themselves you have no sense of the artist behind them. His outstanding quality, as artist and person, is *sanity*. Complete esthetic equipment, all managed by good sound judgment about ways and means, aims and purposes, utilities and 'functions'— and all this level-headed balance-mechanism added to the lively mental state that makes an artist an artist. Fortunate equipment in a disordered world. . . ."